To Bob a very
dear friend
CR

Charles Rich

Autobiography

D0111019

ST. BEDE'S PUBLICATIONS
Petersham, Massachusetts

St. Bede's Publications
P.O. Box 545
Petersham, MA 01366-0545

Printed in the United States of America

96   95   94   93   92   91   90   5   4   3   2   1

LIBRARY OF CONGRESS CATALOGUING-IN-PUBLICATION DATA

Rich, Charles.
   Charles Rich : autobiography.
        p.   cm.
   ISBN 0-932506-80-1
      1. Rich, Charles. 2. Converts, Catholic—United States—
   Biography. 3. Converts from Judaism—Biography. 4. Mystics
   —United States—Biography. I. Title.
   BX4668.R49A3   1991
   282'.092—dc20
   [B]
                                                    90-52664
                                                       CIP

Fifty-two years ago, my friends suggested I write the story of my life, so I asked my spiritual director if I should do so and he said yes. But the trouble was that every time I wrote down a few pages I became very self-conscious so this distracted me from praying and I had to stop. Some time later I tried again, and again the same thing happened, but now that I am nearing the end of my life, I feel it's the duty of everyone who can at all do so, to leave some record behind as to who he was and how good God has been to that person all the time he was on this earth. And so fifty-two years later, I'll try all over again, so here goes:

I was born eighty-six* years ago in the beautiful Hungarian country, as beautiful a country as I was ever in. My mother came from strong Hassidic background and was one of the most spiritual human beings I ever met. Her Hassidic father, she told me, was noted for his charity to the poor and kept open house for Jewish travellers who were too poor for any other kind of lodging. He was also famous for his deep Hassidic piety. I once asked my mother where she got all her beautiful spiritual qualities, and she said she derived from her holy father. She rarely spoke of the influence her mother had on her. My father was in the U.S. so I saw him only once during the first ten years of my life. In the meantime, my mother arranged for me to have the association of holy Jewish men who were not married so that they may in that way devote themselves completely to the study of the holy Scripture and the commentaries made on them by the different Rabbinical schools.

There were no public schools where I lived for the first eight years, so arrangement was made for individual Jewish men to teach a group of boys to read and write in the Yiddish language, the reading consisted in the study of the first five books of the Old Testament known as the Holy Torah. My spiritual life during those early years consisted in attending the morning

*Born 22 April 1899, Charles Rich began to write the Autobiography in March 1985.

prayers which took place in the synagogue, which began before daybreak. Each morning I found myself walking to the synagogue to attend these early morning public prayers so my getting up for Mass now around three or four o'clock is no problem to me. As far back as I can remember, I found going to the synagogue a form of intense delight and prayer became a form of recreation to me and a source of deep joy, making me feel surrounded by supernatural forces. From as far back as I can remember, I never felt myself alone in the world and this even I only had one friend. I felt spiritual forces making themselves my companions and felt being with them wherever I found myself, especially in the beautiful Hungarian forests in which I used to spend hours without any other boys.

At the age of eight, my mother took me to a city where I could get advanced studies in scripture and the commentaries on them, so she made arrangement to stay there for one whole year, till her next visit. At the end of two years, my father accumulated enough money to "import" the whole family to the U.S. Upon my arrival in New York my father took me to a Hebrew school to continue the education. But at the age of ten, I found myself seated with boys twice my age who used to make fun of their teacher, so I left this Hebrew school, and this because there was no serious effort made there to really learn what I went there for. As soon as I got to N.Y. I was immediately registered in a public school; but at the age of thirteen, my father had me get my working papers so I could be of economic help to my destitute family. I worked this way on and off till I was around seventeen or eighteen years old. One day, passing a place in N.Y. known as Cooper Union where lectures were given for those who were unable to go to school, I saw a sign which read as follows: "Was the universe created or manufactured," or words to that effect. Now, not having had any schooling I was totally ignorant of the kind of subjects taught in school, so I determined to attend the first of these talks. When I got inside though, I found I was not able to understand at least eight words out of ten. So I began making notes of the words I did not understand so that by next week I had eight or so words less that I did not understand. It was customary for those who attended these lectures to gather outside after they were over, and make comments on them. As I stood there among these adults I looked at my little notebook and someone near by asked what was in this notebook. After telling him what I did, he showed deep interest in me and we agreed to meet quite often—it turned out that this indvidual by the name of William Hastings was a retired high school teacher from the city of Rochester, N.Y., and unmarried, so he had plenty of time to sort of give me private lessons. As the years went by, we got to know each other with greater intimacy and my knowledge of the world increased with my association with this person.

Now, it turned out that this William Hastings was a confirmed agnostic, though he termed it a polite form of atheism, who harbored deep animosity for all organized religion. He was especially hostile to Christianity, and the Catholic Church. But since I had left off practicing my own Jewish faith when I was fourteen years old, his hostility towards religion did not in the least way disconcert me. All I knew was that this man opened up to me the doors of learning which would have otherwise remained shut to me, and it was the result of this learning that refined my nature which without this learning would have been coarse and crude, to say nothing of its having been vulgar. This relationship kept up for twelve years, and all this time there was not any subject such as philosophy, poetry and prose as well as the plastic arts which was not deeply gone into and discussed. Religion was also a subject of discussion, and it's ironical that a person with his prejudices should have been so deeply concerned with the subject of God. He knew that I was by nature deeply religious, and that I had read extensively along deeply religious and spiritual lines, and especially of all the great classics on mysticism, so he never cast any ridicule on my religious and spiritual interests. In fact, he even had deep regard for the fact of my wanting to get to know God in a personal way, so he one day said these startling words to me: "You have such a strong desire to believe in the truths of faith, that I don't think you'll ever be able to believe in them unless God will Himself come to you and He will Himself speak to you about Himself." Now, these words coming from a confirmed agnostic or a polite atheist, are now, looking back at them, quite startling, because in a very marvellous and extraordinary way, God did actually speak to me years later when I found myself in a Catholic church during which I heard these words spoken in the substance of the soul and in a substantial way, and of which same substantial way St. John of the Cross speaks in his great masterpieces of mystical theology.

To get on with the story of my life. At the age of thirty-three I had read every important literary work held famous in the eyes of men, and yet there was something keenly ill at ease in my spiritual and intellectual outlook. I had even read the writings of the great Christian writers like St. Augustine, St. Thomas Aquinas, St. Bernard, and others as well as those of the saints like St. Catherine of Siena, and St. Teresa of Avila, to say nothing of all the learning of the secular schools. At one time I decided to read everything Shakespeare had written and I did. I also read the sermons of the great Anglican writers like Jeremy Taylor, Cardinal Newman, and a whole host of others which would bore the reader to be into. And yet, as I said, there was distress in my spiritual and intellectual make-up, so much so that I thought of suicide as a way out of the misery, spiritual and intellectual I was in. I felt like a famished person who had not eaten for days and my soul was hungry for the truths of the Christian religion, I did not know how to attain. I had read the Old and New Testaments over and over, and knew passages of them by heart. I was especially impressed by the writings of the four Gospels and was fascinated by the Person of our Lord. But, faith failed me, and I felt that without supernatural faith I could not go on living and this in the same way as anyone would soon die if he was not given food to eat. So despairing of ever arriving at the truths of the Christian religion, I actually went to the Bronx Park with the intention of hanging myself. I had picked out a tree and had a rope in my hand, when someone passed by and courage failed me. I made another attempt to take my life and this also failed. Anyway, I one day passed a Catholic Church—it was a hot summer day, and I felt weary and exhausted. So I thought if I went inside I could cool off. But I was afraid that not being a Catholic, I would be unwelcomed, and this as I was shabbily dressed and unkempt. But overcoming my fears I went inside and found myself completely alone.

This was not the first time I was in a Catholic Church. I used to go quite often to the Cathedral of St. John the Divine and bathe my soul in the beautiful Christian architecture as well as the whole atmosphere of that place. I also made frequent visits in the different non-Catholic churches to be found in Manhattan, so I was not a stranger to things Christian and things Catholic. But my visit to this church was different because I did not go in there to enjoy in its artistic atmosphere. I went into this church because I was weary of my existence, so weary of it, that I even tried to bring it to an unlawful end. I went into that church to find what I had so far been unable to find, something unknown and ineffable, something which would enable me to go on living and not die out of sheer despair.

From now on, the story of my life will take on a delicacy which can hardly be expressed in words of earth, for it has to do with a remarkable experience that took place in my whole spiritual and intellectual make-up during the few moments I kept kneeling in thanksgiving for a favor from heaven I never thought would ever be granted me in the present life, the favor from heaven which enabled me to believe in the divinity of Christ, and with that belief put an end to the misery I went through for a period of so many years—it was as if God Himself came to my rescue that day, and that He Himself spoke to me with His own voice saying to me that Christ is God, fulfilling the prophecy made by my agnostic friend so many years ago when he said to me these words: "You have such a strong desire to believe that you won't be able to do so until God Himself will talk to you," and talk to me He did, during the few minutes that brought such a profound change in me spiritually and intellectually that I have since that time been unable to recognize the self I had been prior to that experience, an experience the full nature of which will only be able to be made known after this life is over, and this on account of the extraordinary nature of that experience, an experience which I felt had to be confirmed by the Church before it could be accepted as coming from God. And it was confirmed by an incident which took place in the following manner: It was my custom to stop in the branch library near my house before going home. So a few minutes after what took place in the church, I found myself in the vestibule of this library looking at a green card posted on the billboard and on it were these words: "The Mystical Christ and the Modern World," a series of lectures to be given by Ignatius W. Cox, S.J., at the Fordham University Chapel on Sunday at 4:00 P.M. I was shabbily dressed, so I dreaded going to the Chapel to hear this talk. But overcoming my diffidence, I found myself seated and saw a priest mount the pulpit. As soon as I heard his voice, I said to myself that he would be the kind of person to whom I would want to relate what took place in the church. I was reluctant to do this because I had never spoken to a Catholic priest since I arrived in N.Y. and in Europe, in the small village I was in, the idea of talking to a Catholic priest would never even occur, so it was for this reason I felt I could never talk with someone like himself, because I never had any formal schooling except three grades of grammar school, I formed an inferiority complex that took years to overcome. But my desire to have this priest's view of what took place in the substance of the soul, was so overwhelming and so tremendous that I went home and wrote Fr. Cox a ten page letter beginning with my life as a young boy in Hungary and ending up with this experience in the church. In this letter I asked Fr. Cox if he had time to talk to me about this experience and if he himself did not have time could he let me know if there was another priest I could talk to about this matter—I felt that everything depended on what a Catholic priest would have to say about such an experience and that without confirmation by him such an experience could not be taken seriously and the whole thing could have been an illusion and deception. Anyway, two days passed and when I looked at my mailbox, I saw the words "Fordham University" on the side of the envelope. I immediately opened the letter and read these words: "Dear Charles, how can I fail to find time to have talks with one to whom Christ Himself has spoken."

It would be almost impossible to express in words what took place in my heart after reading these words, since I felt a weight had been lifted from my soul that I carried about me for so many agonized years, the weight in the form of my inability to believe that Christ was God and that He came on earth to save my soul. A few days later I went to Fordham to meet with Fr. Cox and as soon as we sat down he said these words to me: "You have two whole hours to talk to me and I will not interfere during these two hours." When I got through he placed his arms around me and said, "As long as I am at this university you are free to come here as often as you wish." But as regards the matter of Catholicism he said nothing. In fact, he even went out of his way to assure me that I don't have to worry about becoming a Catholic, and to keep on practicing my Jewish faith as hitherto. After a few days I wrote this letter to Fr. Cox:

I said that seeing that there are other great religions in the world and which same I had studied quite profoundly, like Buddhism, and since there had been other great religious leaders, I did not feel the need to become a Catholic at all. Immediately I got this letter from Fr. Cox: "For you, there is no salvation outside the Catholic Church." and so that was that. I went to see Fr. Cox and he sent me to a priest at St. Francis Xavier on 16th Street to start instructing me. After a few weeks of these instructions, Fr. Corbett said these words to me: "You know," he began, "I feel kind of sad to go on with these instructions, because no one is going to believe you." I replied that I knew no one is going to believe me—I had in mind my Jewish friends—but Fr. Corbett corrected me by saying it is not the Jewish friends, the Catholics are not going to believe you. Anyway, after a few more instructions, he gave me a letter to my parish priest who after reading its contents said to me, "I am going to take my time about these instructions, and I can see you are not satisfied with my answer because you had hoped to be baptized right away." He also told me that he did not think I would come back to him, so if I am received into the Church, I should let him know. After this experience I told a friend of mine who knew Fr. Cox to tell him I am going to stop taking any further instructions, because I believed they did not trust my sincerity. Immediately Fr. Cox sent for me and I went back to Fr. Corbett who gave me a note to Fr. Clark at Fordham. When Fr. Clark came to the parlor we went outside and entered into a two-hour-long conversation on literature. After it was over, Fr. Clark said this to me: "Why did you come to see me?" To which words I replied that I was sent to him for further instructions, whereupon Fr. Clark said you don't need more instructions: you need the sacraments, giving me a note to this effect. I took the note to Fr. Corbett and was baptized on March 18, 1933, thus ending the saga of my life as a member of the Jewish household and making me a member of the Mystical Body of Christ.

Now that I had the grace to become a Catholic at the age of thirty-three, the question came up what I should do with the remaining years it will be God's will for me to stay in this life, and the thought that then presented itself to me was how ideal it would be if I could do so in a monastery.

I had for the first ten years of my boyhood days spent in the company of unmarried religious Jewish men who spent their entire days in the back of the synagogue, in study and prayer, so living among celibates did not at all strike me as strange. So anxious was I to spend the rest of my life in a religious community, that I even told the Jesuit father who was instructing me in the faith, that if the Jews had monasteries I would not have to become a Catholic and that one reason for becoming Catholic was that I would in that way be able to spend the rest of my earthly life in study and prayer. I felt I would be able to do enough work to pay for my board. But God had other plans, because after spending ten whole years trying to become a member of one of the six or seven religious communities I tried to enter, I found it to be God's will I should not be able to fulfill the requirements for such a life. After ten years of such efforts, Fr. Clark told me not to try any further along those lines, and so Fr. Cox, to whom I would go for advice, the first few months in the Church, told me to get a job and do my praying after working hours, and this distressed me to the point of tears, since I could in no way even imagine myself going back to the kind of life before my conversion. I felt that something extraordinary happened to me for the few moments I was in the Church, and which same rendered me something other than I had been prior to that experience. I felt that as the result of that experience, I should give myself completely to God, and that if I could not do so in the environs of a religious community, that I would do so outside of such an environment. I almost said to God that I will give myself completely to Him and it was His job to take care of all my material needs, and Fr. Cox in no way agreed with such a resolve. He even wrote me the following letter if I did not follow his advice and go back to the world to resume the life I lived prior to my conversion. The letter was framed in these words: "You are travelling on a road filled with unlimited dangers." When I read these words I got real scared, so I went to see Fr. Clark and asked him if there was anything dangerous in the manner of my life, and the reply he gave was that there was not. A few minutes after leaving Fr. Clark, I saw Fr. Cox walking on the campus and told him what Fr. Clark said. After hearing this Fr. Cox told me that I should from that moment on never again pay any attention to anything he had to tell me and to go to Fr. Clark for advice. "Compared to Fr. Clark," he said, "I am only a baby."

Needless to assert that that was the last time I went to Fr. Cox for any advice as to how to conduct myself in a spiritual way. One day I said these words to Fr. Clark: I told him that everyone has to have a purpose in his life, whereas there seems to be no purpose at all as regards my way of living, and the reply to this was, "The purpose for which you are living is to say another Hail Mary." Years later I kept calling these words to mind, whenever doubts came to me as to the value of my way of life and whether the kind of life I live is pleasing to God.

One day I spent over two hours in the Fordham University Chapel and after it was over, I got the feeling that maybe I wasted those two and a half hours, seeing I did nothing during that time but feeling myself lost in God. I was afraid because I was not aware I was praying and I would have profited by spending that amount of time at the university library in which I used to stay five or six hours every day. So I went to see Fr. Clark and told him of the amount of time I spent in the chapel without feeling I did anything worthwhile all the time I was there. Was it all right to spent that amount of time, I asked, if I did not pray in a discursive manner? The reply he gave gave deep peace because he said what I did during those two and half hours was in no way displeasing to Our Lord. From that day on I had no scruple as regards spending long hours praying in church though I did not do so in a formal way. I just felt it to be spiritually enjoyable to just sit there and drink in the silence and seclusion of the church's atmosphere and I did not feel the need for analyzing whether what I did was in any way productive from a practical point of view.

I recall along this line an instance in which a priest saw a man in the church spending eight hours at a time in there. The priest did not see this man having a prayer book, so he asked him what he did during those seven or eight hours and the reply this man gave was expressed in these words: "I look at God and He looks at me." From that day on I considered this a perfect answer as regards contemplative prayer, seeing contemplation has been defined as "the look" or "a look of the soul."

Well, to go on with the story and to refrain to bore the reader with the many details of a life like the kind I have been living since the first day of my baptism. I had for years lived by myself, a priest paying my room rent while others gave me enough money for food. After living this way for a while I found myself in the parish of the Paulist Fathers who gave me permission to make use of their library, so I would stay there till late in the night. One day a Paulist Father asked if I ever thought of becoming a priest, and I told him I did not, so he said I should think about this matter. I immediately went to see Fr. Clark about it and he said if I want to study for the priesthood he had no objection. After hearing this I said, "What do you want me to do?" and he said if you want to do want I want then don't study for the priesthood. After I asked him why, he said he did not believe in delayed and late vocations, so this ended the matter for good never again to have to be brought up.

After having Fr. Clark for fourteen years, God took him to Himself so I began going for direction to Fr. Joseph McFarlane, S.J., who after a few sessions with him said he did not believe that anyone with the kind of life I lived should live alone and that he would get me a place with the Jesuit Fathers. I told the pastor of the Paulist church that I would have to leave the parish in which I stayed for ten years, and he said he could give me a room with his community and all I would have to do to get my room and board would be to close the doors of the church each night at nine o'clock. This sounded good to me, so I moved in with the fathers. I used to spend five or six hours each day at St. Peter's Church on Barclay Street where the Blessed Sacrament was exposed after Mass. One day, as I was in my usual way of holding communion with God, I felt myself distracted by the thought that I'd have to close the church, so I tried as hard as I could to get rid of this thought without success, so the next day I told Fr. McFarlane about this and he said I can't close the church so I should tell the pastor about it. The pastor was furious and the community council said if I can't perform such a minute task there must be something amiss with my prayer life, and the type of spirituality I practiced. The decision was that if I cannot close the church I can't live with the Paulist Community, and that I must either follow their advice or that of Fr. McFarlane. To make this story short, arrangement was made with the provincial that I can live here at Xavier and be completely free to follow the bent of my nature and to be free to do as I feel in an interior way.

Something must now be said as regards my prayer life and the kind of books to be read to nourish such a prayer life, since without reading, the kind of prayer its God's will for me to practice would lead to illusion. Along this line does not St. Paul say: "Attend unto reading"? Also in one of the prophetical books we read: "My people were led away captive because they had no knowledge," that is, of God's dealing with the soul and of the soul's dealing with Him. As I said earlier, I had even before my conversion read many outstanding works by saints like St. Augustine. I even carried a copy of his *Confessions* about me for about ten years before I ever thought I'd be a Catholic. But now that I began to pray along contemplative lines, I felt the need to read the writings of St. John of the Cross, St. Teresa, St. Bernard, St. Gregory the Great and to do so over and over, seeing these mystical masterpieces are so profound and so sublime that it's a complete waste of time to read them only once or twice, for they have to be read and re-read dozens if not a hundred times to be of profit to the soul's prayer life, especially a contemplative prayer life. When I became a Catholic I heard some people say everyone should not read the writings of St. John of the Cross, so I went to ask Fr. Clark his view of these writings, and the answer he gave was this: "There is nothing more sublime outside the Sacred Scriptures." When asked whether anyone can read these writings he said yes, but if a person is in serious sin he should read something which will be of help to him to overcome his sin, and if a person is too preoccupied with exterior works that he has no leisure required to profit by such writings. But as for the beneficial effects derived from the writings of St. John of the Cross, of this there can be no doubt and so anyone can and should read them who does not fall in the two above categories.

The problem with relating the story of one's life is to know how to omit those details from it which would be boring to recount. And yet, it's these very details that make up one's life, so to omit them is the same thing as not to say anything about one's life which would be of relevance to the author himself and to those who read about it.

There is one incident in my life which I think would be worth relating and it concerns the writings of St. John of the Cross. I had the habit of spending hours in one of our branch libraries browsing among the books in it. One day I came across a book with this strange title: *The Dark Night of the Soul,* and on opening it up I saw an Imprimatur which made me place this book back on the shelf as I had a feeling that a book with a Catholic Imprimatur was dangerous to read, as it may contain many falsehoods in an intellectual way. I had in those days the same aversion for a book with an Imprimatur as I have today for one without an Imprimatur. Anyway, the next time I found myself in this library, I could not restrain my curiosity as to what a book like this would contain and the reading of it may be of help in my intense quest for truth no matter where this truth can be found. So, I opened the pages and read the description St. John of the Cross gives of the different stages of suffering the soul experiences on its road to finding God in a personal way—as I kept reading the details in it a feeling of fear came over me, because I felt it outlandish that a book like this so foreign to my way of thinking and feeling should describe in detail the experiences I had for years gone through. I could not figure out how a Jewish mentality should find itself confronted with ways of feeling by someone so alien to this mentalilty—I had for years felt that an unbridgeable chasm existed between Christianity and the kind of Judaism I was brought up in from my earliest childhood days. In short, the thoughts I read of in the book repelled me spiritually and intellectually, but for some unknown reason, I was unable to control my curiosity so I kept on reading all of its contents. Would and could I then imagine that the writings of St. John of the Cross would one day become the indispensable mainstay of my prayer life, and that without his writings I could never have lived the prayer life I had the grace to practice for the entire fifty-two years as a Catholic.

I relate this incident to point out how utterly marvellous and extraordinary the life of a human being is, and how wonderful of God to fill that life with His infinite mercies! I have for the past fifty years read and re-read everything St. John of the Cross has written and even got myself an edition of his writings in Spanish, so I could look up some important passage in order to get a deeper insight in it than a translation can give. I have found in the years I have been reading this Doctor of Mystical Theology that what he has to say on the subject with which he deals, are so profound and that they are so sublime that unless they are read over and over dozens upon dozens of time they cannot be understood in a way in which they would be of help and profit to one's prayer life.

So much for St. John of the Cross. There are a whole host of all the other great masterpieces of spirituality written by the Doctors of the Church which I felt not to absorb all they had to say would be inimical to the kind of life it is God's will for me to live, and chief among these are the writings of St. Gregory the Great, especially his commentary on the Book of Job, running into two thousand pages, which I have read and re-read during the course of many years. Then there is the great classic of St. Francis de Sales, his *Treatise on the Love of God*, which has not left my hand ever since it was recommended to me fifty years ago by Fr. Clark.

Fr. Clark had a habit of asking me what books I read, so one day he asked if I had read the writings of St. Francis de Sales, so I said I did and mentioned his *Introduction to a Devout Life*. When I said this to him he said it was the *Treatise* he had in mind when he asked this question, so I said I did glance through it one day and did not find anything in it to particularly impress me, and little did I then think that this work would become one of my favorite books. On hearing me say this, Fr. Clark told me to look through it again sometime, he did not press or urge me to do this but just casually hinted I do so. I could never get over marvelling how such a wonderfully learned and holy person as he was, could put up with my stupidity saying I did not see anything worthwhile in one of the greatest classics of Catholic spirituality. However, I had such deep reverence for Fr. Clark's mind, that I immediately got myself a copy of this book which, as I said never left my hands ever since, and which I must have read over and over so many times that I literally memorized whole passages in it.

Besides the books just mentioned, there was a great *Commentary on the Song of Songs* which I began reading for some time before I even thought of becoming a Catholic, and which since my conversion, I have read and re-read as many times as the books just mentioned. Then there are the writings of St. Teresa and St. Gertrude the Great which have equally become part of my own way of communing with God—with St. Teresa, there developed an almost personal love as if she was actually alive and we met and spoke with each other. I don't think it is at all possible to comprehend the essential nature of Catholic mysticism without absorbing in one's spiritual make-up the books just mentioned, one has to live with these books to really get out of them what their authors intended should be gotten out of them, and which same the Holy Spirit who inspired these authors intended should be gotten from the reading of them.

There can really be no end to the enumeration of all that goes into the make-up of a person's spiritual and intellectual life, so great care must be made to select whatever salient details there are in such a life so as not to make a life tedious to recount and wearying to go through.

The problem one has looking on his life in retrospect, is that there are so many details in it which enumerated one would never get through and the number of them would be wearisome to read. Still, there are certain of these details which cannot be omitted if one is to give an insight as to what took place in one's spiritual and intellectual make-up and one of these details concerns the reading of Goethe's *Faust*.

I had read that after World War I, Goethe's *Faust* was widely read by the wounded German soldiers in the hospitals throughout Germany, and this made me curious about this world masterpiece. I still had enough of the Yiddish language for me to take a chance of wading into the German original of this work. I was at that time in a very perplexed and confused state of mind, wondering and doubting if there is anything at all in the universe on which one could depend for some meaning, and whether there is any good in it that outlasts the evils with which it is so filled. So I got hold of a copy of Bayard Taylor's translation of this great work and came upon these words as they occur in Part I, Scene xxxiii. In this scene Faust asks Mephistopheles as to who and what he was and how he characterizes his nature and being.

> *Faust:* Who art thou then?
> *Mephistopheles:* Part of that Power, not understood,
> Which always wills the Bad, and always works to Good.

After reading these words I felt as if some great universal truth had been revealed to my mind, the result of which causing me to think and feel had I not read these words, I would not have thought and felt. I read further in this great poem and more I did so more I found in it that with which my mind and heart were in deep sympathy. I began to read this poem in German in order to get closer to the heart and mind of him who gave it birth, and I was in no way disappointed. Today, after a span of some sixty years I still read this poem, and find much in it in total harmony with my Catholic belief, and this especially in the closing scenes of this dramatic and epic work. There is one scene in it which has a particular ring to it. It deals with the death of Faust and the devils approach to claim his soul. When Mephistopheles arrived, he found that the angelic beings got there before him and are taking Faust's soul with them into the place of everlasting rest in the world to come, and as they carry his soul upwards with them, the angels sing this song:

> The noble Spirit is now free
> And saved from evil scheming:
> Whoe'er aspires unweariedly
> Is not beyond redeeming.
> And if he feels the grace of Love
> That from on High is given
> The Blessed Hosts that wait above
> Shall welcome him to heaven.

> *Faust*, Part II, Act V, Scene vii

Reading these words one may ask what have they to do with the spiritual and intellectual life led by one who has become a member of the household of the faith? And to this has to be replied that in the quest for truth, nothing of the great masterpieces of the world's literature can be omitted without harm to the soul's spiritual and intellectual well-being and Goethe's *Faust* was one of the stepping stones on which my soul mounted on its road to the possession of the truths I now hold to be so self-evident, the truths namely of my holy Catholic faith. I found many things in *Faust* which confirm the truths I now possess by the aid of God's grace, so if I am to disclose the incidents of my spiritual and intellectual life, all that I find in Goethe's *Faust*, which harmonizes with the truths of my Catholic faith, such instances of this masterwork cannot be omitted.

I still read Goethe's *Faust* and as I do I find no inconsistancy with the truths of my Catholic faith. Not only do I find no inconsistancy with the truths of faith, but I even find them confirming the truth of that faith, like for instance in a line like this: *Das Wunder ist des Glaubens schönstes Kind* (Wonder, or the sense of wonder, is the darling child of faith).

Well, enough of Goethe's *Faust*, although to be fair not enough can be said in reference to the effect this poem had on my mind and heart many years before I became a Catholic. It still does have such an effect on my mind and heart every time I turn to its beautiful thoughts and words. As for reading the great literary masterpieces, are we not told that Moses was versed in all the wisdom of Egypt? Many times I find in Goethe's *Faust* that which could have been said by one of the Fathers and Doctors of the Church, a deep religious insight into the human heart. So God bless Goethe for his assistance to me on my road to eternal happiness and his aid to help me find the truth as this truth of His stands revealed in the nature of things.

Are we not told that "since the creation of the world, his invisible nature, [God's] eternal power and divinity have become visible, recognized in the things that have been made" (Romans 1:20)? The great literary masterpieces of the world are of help to find God's traces in the universe so they should be read with the diligence of which we are capable. For, properly read, they can help us find Him without whom we cannot even exist.

It's for this reason, though, also in an effort to tell the story of my conversion to the holy Roman Catholic faith, I cannot omit whatever has been of help to me in my quest for the truth. Goethe's *Faust* has been such an undoubted help so I must out of gratitude pay tribute to this great poetic masterpiece for the light it shed on my soul long before I ever thought I would one day receive the grace to be able to believe in the truths of my Catholic faith, truths, confirmed in many portions of this great poem and which saying the greatest translation of *Faust* we have in the English language, also holds it does. In his introduction to his translation of this great work, Bayard Taylor has this to say:

> .... But on the whole, the medieval concept of God prevails and underlies all, as in the Gothic sculpture.... The poet's conception of the Almighty Will is the rock on which the poem is built.

Bayard Taylor sums up his comments on *Faust* with these words:

> Faust carries his own cross, but in his unending search for the ideal he is upheld by a spirit greater than himself, whose dwelling is above and beyond as well as on the earth. The earthly bliss and fruit even of Helena and Faust are doomed to destruction. They chant together
>
> > Hard on the heels of joy
> > Follows grim torture (II, iii, 14.13-14)
> > . . . .
> >
> > Not alone for my delight
> > Am I set on this great height.
>
> Faust, too old for enjoyment, learns to know "care," goes blind and dies, but "the everlasting love" is proclaimed in the end: The angels and the beatified youths promise what Faust has sought from the beginning:
>
> > Divinely taught,
> > You may behold,
> > Him whom you honor
> > You shall behold.
>
> The lantern-tower of "sacred poetry" points upward towards the face of Almighty God, who is Eternal Love.

As one keeps reading this over-long commentary on Goethe's *Faust* one may get the wrong notion that this is not the story of my conversion at all. And yet, from a broad and universal look it

most certainly is the story of my conversion, seeing so many
elements have entered into the make-up of my heart and mind
predisposing them for the truths of faith which are now so
blessedly my own and will be my own till the day, or eternity,
rather, when these truths and this faith will give way to sight,
the sight the Beatific Vision will be for all those who while they
lived, yearned and longed for what is of a nature to last forever,
as did Faust and the reason, in spite of his compact with the devil,
finally attained the redemption of his immortal soul. "The traces
cannot, of mine earthly being, In aeons perish,–they are there–"
(Part II, Act V, Scene vi).

Beauty led me to truth. On the first page of Henry Frances
Cary's translation of Dante's *Divine Comedy*, I wrote these words:
"This book has served to Christianize my semitic mentality,"
because as in the case of Heinrich Heine, another Jewish convert,
my own conversion to the Catholic faith was the "passport to
European culture" so that this, the finest translation in English
yet made of *The Divine Comedy*, never left my pocket for years and
years to come prior to my entry into the Church, for in it, I got
my first glimpse of the grandeur and magnificence of Catholicism, Catholicism was in those days not merely a religious belief.
For me, it then represented all that was beautiful and sublime
and ineffable in the teachings of the four Gospels as well as the
Epistles of St. Paul. For me, personally, Christianity and beauty
were in those days the same thing and where one was the other
was also to be found. It was the beauty of Christ's personality
that attracted me to God's Church. I basked my soul in the
beauty of Christ's being, for, is it not written of Christ, "Fairer in
beauty are you than the sons of men" (Ps. 45:3)?

It is this beauty of Christ's being and the Church He founded I
found depicted in *The Divine Comedy* and because it was His beauty
I there sensed, I fell in love with that beauty and thanks to God's
grace, I have never left off falling in love with the beauty of
Christ ever since those arid and painful days outside the household of the true faith.

As I said, it was *The Divine Comedy* of Dante that opened up to
my soul the magnificent grandeur of the teachings of Christ as
they are to be read in the poetic masterpieces of four of the

greatest poets the world has produced—such as Homer, Dante, Shakespeare and Goethe. I have in all of these detected the truths I now have the grace to hold so dear and to cherish more than I do my life itself, for, the life I live would be no life at all, if it was not based on the truth in these great poetic masterpieces and so it was not for nothing I received the grace, that in reference to Dante's poetry, I wrote "This book has served to Christianize my semitic mentality," since that mentality was never the same after soaking my mind and heart in the sublime and beautiful thoughts to be had in this divine comedy as the words in it have been rendered so sweet and dear to our English speaking ears. I said that Cary's translation of *The Divine Comedy* is the best I have so far read made of it in the English language, because in it one is able to find something of the beauty and flavor of the original. And so much so is this the case, that the *Edinburgh Review* not only compared Cary with Shakespeare and Milton, but did not hesitate to claim that Cary "walks not infrequently by the side of his master and sometimes goes beyond him." It is this remarkable translation of *The Divine Comedy* that I began to hold dear and cherish as I did the Holy Scriptures themselves, seeing it did serve "to Christianize my semitic mentality" rendering that "mentality" Catholic to the *core*. And so, when it comes to paying tribute to the influences exerted over my mind and heart the writings of Dante hold a prominent part, as prominent a part as do the writings of Goethe, Shakespeare, Milton as well as many, nay all the other great poetic masterpieces of the world, and poetry, someone said, is akin to the great religious truths promulgated by the Holy Roman Catholic Church, poetry does not contradict these truths, but confirms them in the most beautiful words that can be spoken in this earth.

And so, as I said in the beginning, it was beauty that led me to truth, the truth of the holy Catholic faith, for it was in Dante's *Divine Comedy* I found these truths so beautifully spoken of and being so beautifully spoken of, the great Catholic and Christian truths immediately captured my mind and heart and made that mind and that heart prisoners to the beauty of all Dante has to say in reference to what I now hold dear and cherish more than I do my life itself, namely my holy Catholic Faith for which same, if God would give me the grace, I'd lay down not only the life I now have but as many of them I could have.

And so, in the realm of poetic beauty, *The Divine Comedy* holds first place. It also holds first place in the influence it exerted over my semitic mentality, rendering that mentality other than it had been prior to my reading this great poetic masterpiece. It is now over sixty years since I began reading Cary's translation of *The Divine Comedy* and the breath of its beauty still hovers over my mind and heart, what a grace from God to have been able to saturate my mind and heart in its beautiful English words!

And so I shall always be grateful to God for extending me the grace to love this beautiful poem so much, so much so, as I said, I carried a copy of it about me for over ten years and read dozens of the commentaries that have been made on the meaning and significence of all Dante had in view by writing the way he did, he is a master poet and so all he has to say is in perfect harmony with our holy Catholic Religion, the words he writes enhance that religion and add to the enjoyment of that religion. Has not one of the Fathers of the Church said that the writings of the great secular poets are to the truths of faith, what leaves of the tree are to the fruit that's on it, and so we should avail ourselves of all the beautiful things that have been written by the great literary geniuses like Homer, Dante, Shakespeare, Milton and Goethe since reading the writings of these great poets will serve to enrich our human nature rendering that nature of ours more attractive to those outside the precincts of our Catholic point of view.

One could go on and on citing all the great works of the secular poets which read aright, in the context of all we are asked to believe, and can be of help in the development of our own intellectual and spiritual life, as they were in my own, so I am now grateful for all the beauty they have brought into this life of mine, rendering it other than it had been prior to my acquaintance with these great works of art. Along this line, I remember reading Milton's *Paradise Lost* and the profound effect it had on me and all of this taking place for years before I ever thought of becoming a Catholic and read anew, in the light of my present belief, I find much in *Paradise Lost* in perfect harmony with the teachings of the Church. So much is this the case, that the great English literary critic C. S. Lewis has this to say in his estimate of *Paradise Lost*:

> In so far as *Paradise Lost* is Augustinian and hierarchical it is also Catholic in the sense of basing its poetry on conceptions that have been held always and everywhere by all. This Catholic quality is so predominant that it is the first impression any unbiased reader would receive. Heretical elements exist in it, but are only discoverable by search; any criticism which forces them into the foreground is mistaken, and ignores the fact that this poem was accepted as orthodox by many generations of astute readers well grounded in theology.
> (Preface to *Paradise Lost*, pg. 82)

Before closing this comment on *Paradise Lost* by C. S. Lewis, may I be permitted to add another quote more personal in nature, and it is contained in these words of Lewis:

> In order to take no unfair advantage I should warn the reader that I am a Christian, and that by some (by no means all) of the things which the atheist reader must "try to feel as if he believed" I actually, in cold prose, do believe. But for the student of Milton my Christianity is an advantage.   (Ibid, pg. 65)

What C. S. Lewis just said as regards the atheist reader of *Paradise Lost* can also be stated as regards the reader of Jewish persuasion, since for me too, as a convert to Christian religion, for me too my new found Christian faith is an advantage when it comes to reading *Paradise Lost*.

Someone said these words: "What happiness to be a Catholic even were it for this life alone," and now after having the grace to be one for the past fifty-two years, I can more than confirm the truth of the above words—one day, waiting for the elevator, someone said these words to me: "How's things, Charlie?" The surprising answer made to this question was framed in these words: "I am a Catholic; I can't complain." I said these words surprised me by their stark simplicity and yet they were as profoundly true as if a whole treatise of theology were given as an answer to the question asked. And though it is true, that St. Augustine says "we are Christians only on account of our belief in the Resurrection," it's belief in the Resurrection which is the source of such intense delight all the time we stay in this life thus rendering true what was said of the happiness there is in being a Catholic were it for this life only, thus bringing it the realization what joys they miss who have not received the grace to become the members of the only true faith, since had they received such a grace, they would feel themselves compensated by it for everything else they did not have, since having the true faith, they, with the having of that faith, possess everything worthwhile this side of heaven.

And so, as I look back at all the time it has been my grace to be a Catholic, I can't stop thanking God for his having given me such a favor from heaven, as my faith in the holy Roman Catholic Church is. Along this line, did not St. Teresa of Avila console herself by her oft repetition of these words: "After all, I am a daughter of the Church," feeling that in being "a daughter of the Church" her happiness in heaven will remain assured, and with her happiness in heaven thus assured, what is there in the present life which could disconcert her and fail to render her heart and mind joyous with the kind of delight they experience who are now in heaven?

As long as we will stay in this life it is our faith that will matter, this and no other things in our present form of existence. Of what good would it do for us to be blessed with the possession of this world's goods, if we failed to have the assurance that faith gives us that after this life will be over we will be ineffably and inconceivably happy, and having this assurance, how can one complain if he or she fails to possess what so many foolishly hold in such high esteem, the perishable good things of the present life. For, what are the good things of the present life compared with the ones awaiting us as soon as we close our eyes in death?

But, as one reads all this, what has this to do with the story of my life, as that life has been lived in the Church of Rome for the past fifty two-years? It has everything to do with it; since speaking of all the Church has to offer us we re-tell God's wondrous work in the human soul, filling that soul with His holy truths as these truths of His are promulgated by the Church He has Himself founded. By recounting the wonderful things to be had by the grace of faith, of our own lives, as these lives of ours are one with all we hold dear in a spiritual way, the spiritual way being a Catholic enables one to value and to cherish, what is of a nature to last forever, seeing it's by means of our faith we have the grace to remain joyous in heart and maintain a cheerful disposition, the cheerful disposition which could never have been our own were God not good enough to give us the grace to become the members of His household the Church of Rome will always be. And this as long as there will be a world and men and women in the world. For as long as the world will last, the Church of Rome will never fail to attract to herself those whom God has from all eternity foreknown to become attracted to her, and of this attraction I wish to write in describing the story of my conversion to the only true Catholic faith.

As I said at the outset of this narrative, I was brought up among a pious Jewish sect known as the Hassidim. As a young boy I had the grace to spend a great deal of my time in their blessed society, I say blessed because being with them was to be in the midst of those who gave themselves up to a life of holiness consisting of prayer and study.

It would be too long to enter into the particular details of my life as a boy of eight or ten years old; but it was a life given completely over in the quest for Someone whose presence made itself mystically and ineffably felt in everything around me, such as the forests in which I would spend whole hours of the day meditating on the wonder and mystery I felt all things contained in themselves, and especially in the nature and make-up of a human being. What is a human being, I would often ask myself, and what and who am I? Who is it who made me and all that I find myself to be, and where can I find this Someone so as to thank Him for His having made me all that I am? It was this quest for the Author and Creator of my being, which became an occupation that has never left me until the day I was in a Catholic church and heard the voice of Christ speak in the substance of my soul, saying to me in a substantial way, "Christ is God," and that it is all literally true, all I have read about Christ in the Gospel books. And since all of this has already been recounted in the beginning of this autobiography, I can now proceed to further events and incidents in my prayer life, and the kind of spirituality I have been taught to practice by my holy and learned spiritual director, the Reverend Francis William Clark, S.J., to whom I went for spiritual direction for fourteen years, and who I saw every week during these fourteen years, and who is directly responsible for the kind of a person I have been all the fifty-two years in the Church since it is due to his direction that I got the grace to develop myself along the spiritual lines I have been living all these years as a Catholic. And were it not for Fr. Clark, there is no doubt in my mind I would not today live the kind of life I do, one devoted to study and prayer, since without his wise direction such a life could in no way be lived.

And so, as we go on living, we find it both useful and profitable and consoling to recall all those whose influence on us caused us to become the men and women we have the grace to be. Certainly in my own case, this is very easy to do, seeing had I not had the grace to get to know Fr. Clark in an intimate way, I would in no way be able to account for the kind of life it is God's will for me now to live. Were it not for Fr. Clark's direction, how could I have had the courage necessary to live in such an unusual way, the unusual way of a lay contemplative, since it was for the purpose of enabling people to live lives of contemplation that contemplative orders have been established in the Church, seeing that a favorable environment is necessary to live such a life.

As I said in the beginning, I had for years tried to get into a religious order, there to live a life of study and prayer. But as it turned out, I lacked the qualities to enable me to assume duties connected with being a member of the different religious orders, so my director finally told me to stop trying to enter any religious community, so I spent the first fifteen years of my life as a Catholic, living all by myself. After going to Fr. Clark for fourteen years for direction, God took him to Himself, and so I found another one to take his place, and it was he who told me he did not believe a person like myself should live alone, so he will get me a place with the Jesuit Fathers. And so, as I have already gone into the details along this line, it would be superfluous to repeat them here. Suffice it to assert I have lived with the Jesuit Fathers for the past thirty-five years of my life and have found them to be the happiest ones I have so far experienced this side of heaven. My relationship with them being of a unique kind, so it's difficult to speak of it in precise terminology. The day may come when I will be able to relate in words the nature of the relationship here with the Fathers, but so far I have found this relationship to be too unusual to find words with which to speak of it, and I feel it is only in the next life the full account of my life here will be able to be properly expressed. As I said in the beginning, when I first became a Catholic I kind of said these words to God. I told Him I will give myself completely to Him, so it is for Him to take care of my material needs, and He has taken care of these needs for the past fifty-two years I have been in the Church, since I have for the past fifty-two years been able to give myself up to a life of study and prayer, Fr. Clark absolving me from the obligation of earning my livelihood, due to severe physical illnesses, with which I became afflicted as soon as I entered the Church. Sometimes, people hearing me living this way, question the validity of a life like mine, and so when this happens, I call to mind the words of Fr. Clark who, in response to the question I asked as to the purpose for which I live, said, "You live for the purpose of saying another Hail Mary."

I realize these words have already been quoted, but due to their unusualness, they are worth repeating over and over, since that is the purpose for which everyone of us should live, there not existing a higher and nobler reason for our being in this world than the one the glorifying Jesus and Mary is.

One thing that puzzled me during the first years I was in the Church, was how few Catholics there were who wanted to talk about heaven, and how fewer still wanted to go there, and I thought how strange it was for this to be, since if there was a heaven why not want to go there and why be content to stay in a world like this, filled as this world is with the vast amount of sin and evil, and the sufferings issuing from these sins and from this evil. In this connection I recall a very holy Jewish convert telling me that as soon as she got the grace to believe in Christ, she did not want to live anymore. From then on, her main desire was to be with Christ in the state of glory and that with St. Paul, she to wanted to be freed from this life and to be with Christ, and all of this in such direct contrast to what so many Catholics feel. They feel as if it was almost an impropriety even to mention the name of heaven, let alone the desire to go there and looking forward to our departure from this life as a grace from heaven. As for the word eternity, how rarely is this name mentioned among Catholics today, so it was for this reason I asked my director where to go among Catholics, and among what kind of persons I should be in order to be of profit to my soul, and this is what he said to me. He said that wherever I find myself and do not hear the word eternity mentioned frequently, that was no place for me to be, and along this line did not St. Francis de Sales say to the nuns he was directing: "We do not think enough of eternity." And is it not due to the fact that eternity is so rarely spoken of in the churches today, why there are so many defections from the faith. If eternity is not real to men, why bother to make the many sacrifices God asks of us in order that we may one day be with Him in the state of glory? If heaven does not exist why be a Catholic, and if heaven does exist why want to remain on this sad earth with all the many miseries to be had upon it?

All of this puzzled me when I found myself in the Church. I wondered why so few among its members want to go to heaven, and the kind of looks I received every time the word heaven and the joys that are there awaiting us was mentioned by me. To this day I find the whole thing puzzling and perplexing, and yet I have no intention to stop talking about heaven and the joys that are there laid up for us. And, is it not the very thought of heaven, and the hope of our one day going there that makes us want to become Catholics, since the Church alone speaks of the joys that are there, and she does so by the writings of her saints. Was it not this very thought of heaven's joys, and the hope I have of my one day entering into them, that made me become a Catholic, and would I have become a member of the Mystical Christ if there were not such joys to hope for, as soon as we departed from this life, seeing that if we live the right kind of lives, we go to heaven immediately when we leave this world. Yes, it is the hope of heaven's joys that drew me to the Church, and have kept me in her all of these fifty-two years. How sorry we should feel for those who lack the grace to live solely for the things of the next life, and not for the paltry pleasures to be had in time.

Yes, with St. Augustine we say we are Christians on account of our belief in the Resurrection of Christ and for that reason only, seeing that any other reason for wanting to become a Catholic does not make any sense, and a person has to be devoid of their right mind to become a Catholic and not live for heaven alone, since not to live for heaven alone is not to be a member of the household of the true faith at all, and so it's no wonder that with the loss of one's hope in the joys of the life to come, such a person immediately takes leave of the Church, and he turns out to be the enemy of the friend he had once been when the other world was real to him and this world unreal.

Yes, I was puzzled when I was among Catholics and found they rarely, if ever spoke of the joys of the life to come, since it was these very joys that drew me to the Church. It was these very joys that made me love the Church for her promising them to me, if I should abide by her teachings, for it's these joys I crave, and not the false pleasures to be had in time, and which same bring so much pain in their train.

On becoming a Catholic, my aim was to enjoy my new found faith and not to spend time arguing about it with those who will always remain unfavorably disposed to the truths Christ brought into this world. Time, I felt, was too short which was left for me to enjoy the grand and beautiful truths of the Roman Catholic Church. I held my own contribution to these truths was to enjoy and love them with every fibre of my intellectual and spiritual being. Does it not say, "You shall love the Lord thy God" with everything in oneself, and what is the specific aim of this commandment save that we should expend our whole heart's love on the truths of our holy Catholic religion, since to love the Church is the same as to love God by whom she was founded from all eternity, seeing the faith we now hold is as ancient as the world itself, since God has from all eternity foreknown all those who are destined to be the members of the Mystical Body of Christ.

And so, it was my aim not to argue about my new found faith but to love and enjoy it more than anything else to be had in the present life, seeing that anything to be had in the present life will one day cease to be, whereas the Church of Rome will be here forever—the truths she teaches will never cease to be cherished by those whom Christ has called to close union with Himself, seeing it is Christ we love when we love the Church, He and the Church constituting one Person. I became a Catholic so I may thereby receive a taste on earth of what the joys of heaven are like, the truths the Church teaches constituting that taste.

I became a Catholic so that I may in that way spend the remaining earthly days in the kind of happiness and peace of soul to be had in the Church alone and nowhere else on this wide earth. I became a Catholic so that I may in that way receive a partial experience of all they enjoy who are now in heaven—it is heavenward to which the Church points and so it is for this reason I love her so much. I did so because she speaks to me of the eternal life our Lord came to bring. Does He not Himself tell us this when in one of the Gospels He says: "I came that you may have life and you may have this life to the full"?

He most certainly does tell us this and so it's for this reason we are so grateful to God for His giving us His "Only-Begotten Son" to love and to cherish as we do nothing else God has made, seeing we live for Christ alone and that apart from the Life He Himself is, there is no life at all, not the kind that will last forever. "I am the Way, the Truth and the Life," He says to us and we find the Way, the Truth and the Life which Christ is in the holy Roman Catholic Church, and finding him in the Church we have for her become unique and exceptional in a way nothing else on this earth is unique and exceptional—I realized all this when I became a Catholic and, realizing it, I got the grace to yield up my whole heart's love for the institution known as the holy Roman Catholic Church, of which Church Fredrick Ozanam had this to say: "I have known the difficulties of belief, but my own experience has taught me that there is neither rest for the mind nor peace for the heart save in the Church and in obedience to her authority." I too have known the difficulties of belief and I too have found that there is neither rest for the mind nor peace for the heart save in the Church and in obedience to her authority.

And so, as the story of my life as a Catholic proceeds on, it becomes increasingly clear and evident to me that all I now am I owe to the Catholic Church and that without faith in all she teaches I could not go on living. For, without these truths my life would be no life at all but a kind of death that will never have an end. With me, it's either being a Catholic or not being at all, since for me life and Catholicism constitute one and the same thing. For me, to live is Christ and without the Life He is, there can be no existence worthy of the name. As the result of being a Catholic, "I live, nay, not I, Christ lives in me." He does so in the kind of life that will never end, and which same Life He Himself is and the joy of which we receive a taste on earth.

I have thus far omitted a very important incident in the story of my conversion, one that has to do with my devotion to the Blessed Virgin and how this devotion began. It began immediately after being received into the Church. I then lived at home and experienced all the hostility which Jewish people feel towards a convert to Christianity, and especially Catholic Christianity. I have so far not met many, if any, Jewish converts to Protestantism nor have I heard of their being persecuted by their co-religionists for their defection from Judaism; but I have known many who have undergone bitter hatred and animosity for having joined the Church of Rome. Anyway, due to my conversion I found myself terribly alone, having lost the friendship of every single Jewish person I had all my life known, while at the same time not being a Catholic long enough to form new friendships, so I sought for this friendship in a purely supernatural way. There was a church a few blocks from where I lived in the Bronx named after St. John Chrysostom. One day, finding myself in the basement of this church, without a soul present in it, I noticed a beautiful life-like statue of the Blessed Virgin, so I went over and kneeled down in prayer. After finding myself doing this for several hours I felt I was not kneeling at a statue but at the feet of a living human being, and, realizing I am in the presence of someone who is alive, I began pouring out my heart and the desolation I felt at all I had gone through as the result of becoming a Catholic. I poured out to her all the anguish of my soul and as I did so, I felt tears flowing down my face, in thanksgiving for having someone to talk to in this remarkable manner.

For the period of many months after my first visit to the basement of this church, I went there each day of the week and

spent as much as seven or eight hours at the foot of this remarkable life-sized statue, not a statue but some heavenly human
being who was too wonderful for me to even try to understand.
Anyway, here is where I found what I could not find anywhere
else. After keeping this up, as I said, for many months, I one day
left the statue and went to the middle of the altar where the
Blessed Sacrament was reserved.

I have since wondered why I did not go to the place where the
Blessed Sacrament was reserved right away, and not after
months of praying before the statue of the Blessed Virgin and
the answer that now comes to me is that it was my love for Mary
and the delight experienced being near her all these months that
procured for me the grace to acquire devotion to our Lord's
sacramental Presence on the altar.

With my devotion to Mary a new kind of relationship took
place in my mind between God and myself. There was a warmth
about this relationship which can only come about from a personal love for the Great Mother of God, and from a love for her
to the regard I acquired in reference to the women I met as a
Catholic, because I had acquired the false notion that women
were not on the same par with men when it came to the creative
arts. So I one day asked Fr. Clark what the advantages are, if any,
in reading the writing of women saints like St. Gertrude and
others, and he said that there is a depth of feeling in the writing
of saints like St. Gertrude and an unction that would enrich my
interior life. So from that time on I began to have a special kind of
love for the writing of all the women saints and have since then
placed them on the same par with those of St. Augustine, Thomas Aquinas, St. Gregory the Great, St. Bernard, St. John of the
Cross, St. Frances de Sales and others equal to them. I have not
stopped reading St. Gertrude for the past fifty years and have no
intention doing so. Along with this attitude towards women
saints I asked Fr. Clark the view I should have to women in
general and he said it should be no different than the attitude to
men, and that I should have no scruple in forming associations
with women. As the result of this Christlike attitude, I have
acquired the intimate friendship of women who are undoubted
saints, two of whom are members of a religious order and one

who is in the lay state, married and has three children, Ronda Chervin, whom I met twenty-five years go, and a convert from Judaism like myself. This friendship with her is as intimate as any I have had with another human being, and all of this due to the fact that I have all these years held her to be an undoubted, saint, although she never fails to protest my including her in the category of God's chosen ones and of the dearest friends our Lord has on this earth.

Someone whose affection for me is as great as that of anyone now walking this earth, suggested that I should, out of gratitude to God, mention the friends He gave me to replace the ones I lost by becoming a Catholic. So I have to begin with the greatest of these through whose wise and holy direction I became someone totally different than I had been prior to getting to know him in an intimate way, the Reverend William Clark, S.J., and of whom I had written the following on the day I found out he had passed to his eternal reward:

> There was something about Father Clark that charmed and fasci- nated me from the first instant that God in His goodness and love brought me to him. There was an air of exaltation about his whole being; you were made to feel that he lived and moved in realms such as only the blessed inhabit. He reminded me of those who are already in heaven because he was far removed from those many things which occupy most people and distract them from the contemplation of God. . . . He lived and moved in an atmosphere that was charmed and influenced by what cannot be found in the lives of others who are not saints. . . .
>
> I often try to call to mind those wonderful evenings that I spent in his presence and the things we discussed. It was a conversation wholly spiritual and its theme was eternity. . . . Fr. Clark succeeded in evoking hopes and longings only prayer can stir up, so that to be with him for a time was like being close to God.
>
> There was an atmosphere, a radiance, an influence that made one believe that he had access to things hidden and unknown to me. He was in his old age like a great sage, a tower of strength, with some- thing of the force of the Fathers and Doctors of the Church. You went to him with the confidence of one approaching a saint whose insight into the hearts of men was colored with heavenly vision.

As a recent convert to the Church, I once asked him where and to what places I should go in order to profit myself spiritually, and here is what he said: "Wherever you may find yourself to be and you do not hear the word 'eternity' mentioned frequently during the day, that is no place for you to be."

There were of course so many others whose influence exerted on me was such that without their influence I would not today be the person I am. And one of the very first of these is Ignatius W. Cox who was the first Catholic priest I met on this earth and who confirmed the experience I had in a Catholic church as being from God. This whole incident is recounted in a book I had written years ago entitled *Reflections from an Inner Eye*. It would be too long to mention in detail what has there been written, but there is one thing he said which I never failed to thank God for. I had had a very unusual experience of God and felt I actually heard the voice of Christ speak to me in the substance of my soul, so I wanted this experience confirmed by the Church. I did not feel he was in a position to find time to have talks with someone like myself, so I wrote and asked if he could not find such time, could he suggest someone else to whom I could speak about one of the most extraordinary experiences in my whole life and which same took place during the few moments I spent in a Catholic church—I was afraid that what took place in the depth of my inner being might be an artifice of the hater of men, Satan. Well, a few days after having written Fr. Cox, I received a letter opening with these words: "How can I fail to have time to have talks with one to whom Christ Himself had spoken?" Needless to state, these words coming from a Catholic priest, put all my fears of being deceived away and this for the remainder of my life as a member of the only true Church.

There are so many others to whom tribute should be paid for watching over and guiding me spiritually and intellectually during the first few years in the Church, that it would tax the reader to have to read all that can and should be said in reference to the help and affection I received from their holy friendship.

There comes a time in the life of every human being when he or she has to make a choice and this choice consists in being content to remain confined to the limited intellectual, spiritual and cultural environment in which that human being finds himself or to universalize his thoughts and his feelings, so as to in that way transcend the limits in which that person finds him or herself. There comes a time when the quest for universal truth must be uppermost in one's mind and to follow that truth no matter how it will leave him. To me, personally, there came such a time. I had to choose between remaining in the Jewish intellectual, cultural and spiritual environment or to take the risks involved in getting out of such an environment into the broad expanses of the human mind. I had to choose between remaining among my Jewish friends or risk losing them by searching for the truth wherever that truth will lead me. As a matter of fact, as soon as I began occupying my mind with Christian writings I was told by my Jewish friends that if I did not give up reading the writings favorable to things Christian I would find myself alone by losing all those by whom I was loved and cherished so deeply and whom I also loved and cherished. I thought about this and concluded that the truth must be paramount in the life of a human being and that it is better to love the truth than to live without the truth.

In short, it is the truth I had grown to love, so there was not the slightest intention to abandon that truth out of human respect and the comforts I would lose by holding on to the truth, the truth that every human being is equal in the eyes of God and that it is only in the Christian religion one could find true freedom of spirit. Along this line, are we not told that "if the Son of Man will make you free, you will be free indeed"? It was this spiritual and intellectual freedom I sought, instinctively realizing that without such freedom life is not worth living. I had seen there were a large number of religions in the world and that Judaism is only one among these religions, so it lacks universality of outlook. What my soul craved was a religious outlook on life that embraces every single human being who has ever been born into this world and that there was such a religion founded by Christ and promulgated by the Church established by Him. Being both Jewish and Christian I could not be, seeing the tenets of Christ are not those of the synagogue abandoned by Him. Along this line, I am thinking of a great Jewish convert by the name of the Venerable Mary Paul Libermann. This young Jewish man of about twenty-three was about to be ordained rabbi to follow in the lead of his own famous rabbinical father. One day, this Jewish young man said these words: "God of Abraham, Isaac and Jacob, let me know if the Christian religion is true or false." Needless to say, the answer to his prayer came to him at once and he is now being proposed for beatification. A story like this has a profound effect on an enlightened Jewish mentality so it naturally had this effect on my own Jewish way of thinking and feeling, for like Libermann, I too asked God to let me know if the Christian religion is true, and I kept asking this question for a great number of years and did so in everything I read as regards the religion of the God Man. For years I kept wondering as regards the great truths of the Christian religion, and as I did so, the light of its truth gradually began to penetrate my inmost being, that inmost being denoted by the Hebrew word for "heart," for as far as things spiritual are concerned it is the heart, the inmost self of a person, that matters. For does not Pascal say that the heart has reason of its own of which the intellect knows nothing about?

I was searching for the kind of truth that embraces every single human being who was ever been born into this world and so no limited intellectual and spiritual outlook would ever be able to satisfy my mind. I wanted to know if the Christian religion is true, since if it was true, how can I remain in the limited intellectual and spiritual environment of the religion of Judaism into which God gave me birth. I had to make a choice and this choice consisted in universalizing my mind and heart so that that mind and that heart could become capable of embracing every single human being that now walks this earth. I had to make the choice of thinking in universal terms and these universal terms have been established by Christ. They are being promulgated by the Church founded by Him.

The story dealing with a person's conversion is long and it intertwines itself in all kinds of ramifications, so it is practically impossible to trace out all the details of one's spiritual and intellectual life to enable him to account for the way he now thinks and feels in a spiritual and intellectual way.

The autobiography has come to a standstill, so the temptation presents itself as to whether it should go on, because the feeling that comes over a person is whether it is either wiser and possible to record events and incidents in one's personal life which have long since vanished. But there is always a but, and often this but can be used for a good purpose, it is always possible to tear up what one has written, and no loss of any kind ensues. Besides we always enjoy reading about the lives, both famous and infamous, of those who lived before we were born, so how do we know that if someone who lives after we die won't find it both pleasurable and even edifying to read about our own selves, and with this fact before us, have we a right to deny those who come after us the pleasure and help reading about us would procure for them, and is this not really an act of selfishness, depriving us of an opportunity to practice Christian charity? And so, with this in view, I'll try to go on where I have left off, and this will be no easy matter since I have long since forgotten many things I have said about myself, so there exists the risk of repeating what has already been written. But, as I said, there is no harm in trying, so here goes again:

As regards the most salient facts about my life, this I will never cease to remember. I will always call to mind that prior to my entry into the Church, I was so miserable that I made two unsuccessful attempts to end my life and that since the day of my baptism fifty-two years go, I have been so happy in Christ that I would not exchange this happiness for all the wealth and pleasures not only of this world, but for all the other worlds one can imagine may exist. Compared to the joy St. Paul had in Christ, he counted the whole of this world's goods nothing but so much rubbish.

Here we must make room for an analogy. Supposing a person was brought back to this life after having enjoyed the things of Christ in the state of beatitude. Would such a person for even one second listen to us if we talked to him about the pleasures we have in common with the lower animals, such as eating, sleeping and procreating? Would he not look down with the utmost contempt on such pleasures and pity those who have to have them? And, along this line, has not someone said that "the angels pity us." The angels pity us for our having to have what makes this life possible and even livable. Well, it is in some such way I look back on the life I led prior to conversion—I sometimes even wonder how I was even able to live in this world without the possession of Christ in it. How it is possible to go on living without faith in Christ is something I cannot now understand. It is a grace I no longer possess. Now the same thing as regards our need for the Person of our Lord, there is the equal and indispensable need for the possession of faith in the Church which Christ founded, seeing that, in the words of St. Gregory the Great, "Christ and the Church constitute one Person," so where the one is there the other is also. And, important as it is to believe in Christ Himself, it is equally important to believe in the Church He founded and not only believe in the Church but to love her as we do Christ Himself, she constituting his Mystical Body and Bride.

Well, I have already gone further than I thought I would go, so thanks be to God for His having taken me this far on the journey recollection of the past is. I said that prior to my conversion I was one of the most miserable human beings walking this earth and that now, thanks to God's grace, the exact opposite is true and that I would not exchange the happiness I have for the pleasures of even ten thousand worlds, seeing there can be no proportion between a good that is finite and one infinite in range and extent.

Only last night, I spoke to someone who read that the teen-aged daughter asked her enormously wealthy father if he was happy. Upon hearing this I told this person that no matter how well-off materially a person may be, he or she cannot be happy, seeing that it is in Christ alone that happiness can be found and the father of this teenaged daughter, not having Christ, how could he say he was happy? The point of the whole matter is that the teenaged daughter never received a direct answer to the question she asked, and that her father did his best to avoid such a direct answer, knowing in his inmost self that not being able to believe in Christ, he is devoid of the fundamental requisite for the kind of happiness it is possible to have in the present life. And I too, as I look back at my life prior to the time I got the grace to become a Catholic, I too have found myself in the same category of this teenaged daughter's father, because I too, if asked if I was happy would then have been unable to answer this question in the affirmative.

And so, as the world keeps rolling on, it becomes clearer and clearer that there are only two kinds of people in this world, those who have the grace to believe in the truths of the Christian religion, and those who, for reasons known only to God, are devoid of such a grace. And, not having the grace to be able to believe in the truth of the Christian religion how can such people say they are happy in the way and manner God would have them be happy, that is, by finding their whole meaning and purpose Christ can alone be for a human being?

And so, as regards writing an autobiography, there is one single purpose I have in view, and that is to let others know of the joy and delight I have experienced as the result of my becoming a Catholic. I want to announce this joy and this delight from the housetops, so to speak, so that others who are not yet members of the only true Church, may hear of this message so that they too may avail themselves of the grace to become what I have had the grace to become and which as the result of this grace, I have become one of the happiest human beings now walking this earth. I said "one" because there are countless others to give testimony to the same thing.

Do you wish to know what the joys of heaven are like?—I imagine myself saying to those outside the Church, then ask God for the grace to become what I have had the grace to become, seeing if you do this, if you get such a grace you won't have to wait for death to get to know by personal experience what the joys of heaven are like. You will receive a taste of these joys right here on this earth, and this in the same ways as did all of God's saints. All of God's saints have received a taste on earth of what the joys of heaven are like so that by becoming a Catholic, those outside the fold can receive the same kind of taste, a taste which renders us beside ourselves with gratitude to God for his condescension to give us such a taste of himself. It is then, after we get the grace to become Catholics, we will truly and fully understand the words of the Psalmist in which he says to us, "Taste and see how good [Hebrew: sweet] the Lord is."

St. Augustine said that he would rather read what others had written than to write himself, and I feel the same way as regards this autobiography. But, as I said in another part of this narrative, we like to read what others have written, and who have done so before we were born, so in the same way there will be countless others who will enjoy reading what we have ourselves written and it would almost constitute a lack of charity, if out of sheer selfishness, and indifference, and inconvenience to ourselves, we would refrain from at least making some effort to leave some memories of our life for others to be able to read and even be helped by what they read. Also along this line, does not St. Paul tell us to attend unto reading? Also we have the great St. Francis de Sales telling us that in his famous *Treatise on the Love of God,* he "had written nothing he had not learned from others," and this means that some of the greatest spiritual and literary classics would never have existed save through the written word. It is with this in view, that I feel I should make an effort to put down in writing at least some of the things in my life which have served to bring about the state of mind I have been in during the last fifty-two years as a Catholic—the only problem being, that there are so many facts and incidents in that life that it would be impossible to record them all and so only the most salient among them can be enumerated.

Among the many Jewish friends I had, there was one individual who asked why I became a Catholic. Was it some sort of misfortune that prompted this kind of action, or some other factor in my life? I said that "I found Judaism inadequate to the needs of my life," and that these needs were of an intellectual and spiritual nature, to which words he gave this response: "I never before heard this kind of a reason for becoming a Catholic." There are also the words of the Venerable Mary Paul Libermann, who at the age of twenty-three was about to be ordained a rabbi, said these words: "God of Abraham, Isaac and Jacob, let me know if the Christian religion is true." We don't know the exact nature of the answer he received but he from that minute on, got the grace to become a Catholic and this in spite of the bitter hatred his conversion incurred on the part of his father who was also a rabbi.

I mention all this because of the effect the conversion of devout and holy Jewish people had on me, indicating I was not alone with spiritual and intellectual problems which Judaism could not solve and this due to the lack of universality of the Jewish religion, because as I grew in years, I found my mind expanding into intellectual and spiritual realms outside the confines of Judaism. I began to read, as I said, the great literary masterpieces of the world and found myself spiritually and intellectually at home in the realms of these intellectual and spiritual masterpieces, so that my mind and heart felt at home wherever there were human beings, regardless of their spiritual and intellectual views, so that it was the very universality of the Christian Catholic truths that won my heart and my mind and not any other limited kind. There is the case of Heinrich Heine who some say is the greatest lyric poet since the ancient Greeks, saying these words: "My baptism was my passport to European culture." I had cultural needs Judaism was incapable of satisfying and this due to the lack of universality of that religion.

There are so many things to be said along this line, but it would take too much space to mention them all in the limited form of an autobiography. Sufficient to state, that it was in Catholicism my mind and heart found the kind of homeland in which I felt I could spend the rest of my earthly days with the kind of happiness and peace to be had in nothing else this world has to offer, be this good and beautiful in the eyes of some, as it may, because for me, it was Catholicism or being intellectually and spiritually homeless and orphaned. The poet Rilke wrote these words: *Keine Heimat zu haben in der Zeit* (to have no homeland in time). I can say *"Keine Heimat zu haben"* save in the Church of Rome, so I can never stop bragging about such a great favor from God and boasting and shouting with joy at the realization of all that I now am as the result of God's grace one of the most peaceful and joyous human beings now walking this earth. I said peaceful and joyous because that's what the Church has to offer, and in which offer she can have no competitors, since where else outside this Church can we have the peace our Lord came to bring when he said "Peace is my farewell to you, my peace is my gift to you: I do not give it to you as the world gives peace" (John 14:27).

What our Lord is here saying has been repeated by the Church with whom, in the words of St. Gregory the Great, she constitutes "one Person," and it was this peace I received when I became a Catholic, a peace, as we said, no other institution on this earth is capable of conferring, but he only who St. Bernard says "is our peace." For Christ is the peace of the soul, even as he alone can be the spiritual and intellectual home of a human being, there being no other kind of refuge in a spiritual and intellectual way save the one he is.

It is in this spiritual and intellectual homeland I entered the day I got the grace to be able to believe in all that the Church teaches. She it was who became the "*Heimat*," the homeland of the soul, to use the beautiful words of the Austrian poet. In the eighth chapter of Jeremiah we find these startling words:

Peace, peace! they say
though there is no peace.

There can be no true peace without the Peaceful One our Lord is, and so to possess the peace He alone can be for each human being we have to be the joyous and peaceful members of the Church founded by Him.

I know full well, this is not the right way to recall the events of one's life by means of an autobiography. But as one goes on living, one finds nothing this life is to be a this or that thing, everything in it being too complex to be neatly categorized. The same is true writing the story of one's spiritual and intellectual experiences, they too, are too interwoven to be neatly categorized. All that can be said along this line, which will make sense to those who read about this, is to state that as the result of my becoming a Catholic I felt myself spiritually and intellectually at home in the Church of Rome and that I cannot conceive how I could be more at home in any other intellectual and spiritual world than the one the Church has been for the nineteen hundred years of her existence in time, I say her existence in time, because in the eyes of God she always was, in that the Church of Rome existed in the patriarchs and prophets of the Old Testament, since it was of her they spoke in everything they said and did. It is in this Church whose roots extend into eternity, I have had the grace to be a member of, and for which membership I shall never be able to thank God enough, because, whereas before my conversion I was homeless in an intellectual and spiritual way, I have since then found the *"Heimat"* of which the poet Rilke speaks. In the seventh verse of Psalm 68, we read these words: "God gives a home to the forsaken." In the Hebrew, these words read that God gives a home and dwelling place to the lonely in an intellectual and spiritual way, the intellectual and spiritual way they are lonely who for reasons known only to God, have not yet received the grace to become the blessed members of the household of the only true faith.

One of the innumerable attractive features of the Catholic Church consists in the saints she has given to the world. What other religion has produced a St. Augustine, a St. Thomas Aquinas, a St. Bernard, a St. Francis of Assisi, a St. Francis de Sales who wrote these words of his namesake: "God gave to St. Francis of Assisi a view of the world as a miracle of love." God not only gave such a view of the world to St. Francis; He gave this kind of view to all the other saints the Church has produced. He gave such a view of the world to St. Catherine of Siena, to St. Teresa, to St. John of the Cross, to St. Catherine of Genoa and to the thousands upon thousands of the men and women who had attained to the highest state of union with God it is possible to attain under the conditions of the present life, and the saints alone fulfill the conditions to be pleasing to Christ in the way and manner His Father in heaven wishes them to be pleasing to Him, so it is for this reason the saints have made such an impact on my spiritual and intellectual life, for where can be found someone with such a beautfiul outlook on the world as the saint has, who has indeed a "view of the world as a miracle of love," so it is for this reason the hearts of all mankind are turned to the saints with a love and devotion they have for no other human beings. It is not the man of learning, the educator or any other professional man and woman who capture the love of our hearts in the same way as do all of God's saints and which same the Church of Rome has so far produced, for, as we said, to what religion other than the only true one that Catholic religion is, can we go for an Augustine and the other great spiritual and intellectual giants known as the saints of God?

Of one thing in this life we can be certain. We can always be certain of the fact that God will always inspire men, women and even children to turn completely to Him and to give Him their whole hearts and their whole minds. There will always be those who will hold nothing back from God but give Him their entire being, body and soul, and as long as this will be the case, we have nothing to fear from the enemy of the human race who, if there is one thing he dreads it is to see men and women give themselves up entirely to love for Christ. As long as there will be saints in this world, it will continue to be a fit place to be inhabited because were there not a St. Francis in the world it would be the exact same as if there was no physical sun to light it up and to provide us with the needs we have to stay on this earth in a physical way, and when the Psalmist writes

O Lord, our Lord
how glorious is your name over all the earth!...
When I behold your heavens, the work of your fingers,
the moon and the stars which you have made

(Ps. 8:1-4)

he is in a mystical way referring to God's saints, for they are the heavens, intellectually and spiritually speaking, seeing in a figurative way, the saints denote all that is lovable in a human being. Along this line does not St. Bernard tell us that "The soul of every just person is a heaven all by itself"? He most certainly does do so, so it is for this reason I found myself so attracted to the Church of Rome in whom alone can be found men and women of the caliber of a St. John of the Cross and a St. Teresa, so we will look in vain for such spiritual and intellectual giants outside the Church of Rome. And, while it will always remain true that we will find holy men and women outside the Church, none of them have risen to the heights of love for Christ as did all of the saints the Church has seen fit to raise up to her altars, to be revered in an unstinted way, that is, with everything in ourselves, since it is they, the saints who attract to themselves the minds and hearts of the noblest members of the human race. It is not the philosophers of the world to whom we turn for light and inspiration nor to any other class of people, it is to the saints of God we turn in our direst needs and to help us walk in the footsteps of Christ, they, the saints, have walked in His footsteps so they will teach us how to do so too—we need guides to show us the way to heaven and they constitute those guides. Also, do we wish to know what the joys of heaven are like? For this too, we must go to God's saints, since to them had been given a taste of these joys, and seeing them filled with such delight as the result of the taste they have received of heaven's joys, we too will petition God to give us the same kind of a grace, so that we too will receive on earth a taste of what the joys of heaven are like. And, seeing the saints filled with so much ecstatic delight as the result of their being closely united with Christ, I too petition God that if it pleases Him to give me the grace of becoming a saint and to do this by enabling me to become a member of the household of the faith the Church of Rome is. It is by becoming a Catholic, I felt, I can become a saint, by this and in no other way.

And so, as we look about us, we wonder which kind of profession and vocation we should choose and which profession will give us the greatest amount of peace and joy, and, as we do so, we find it is the saints alone that can do so, they alone can procure for us the greatest amount of happiness it is possible for a human being to have and, seeing how happy and how peaceful the saints are as the result of their being close to God, we too ask for the grace to be imitators of the saints, so that with St. Ignatius Loyola we say: "If St. Francis could do this why cannot I?" If the saints had the grace to become the happy and joyous human beings they became, why cannot we do so too? Seeing that in the words of the prophet Isaiah, "God's hand is not shortened," so that what He has done for others, He can do for us as well and it but remains for us to be men and women of "desire." Besides, does He not say in one of the Psalms "Open wide thy mouth and I will fill it," and by "mouth" is here designated one's capacity and desire, since it is in order to become saints we have been born, for this and no other purpose. We have not been born for this or for that thing: we have been put on this earth so that by remaining on it, we may get the grace to dispose ourselves for all the gifts of body and mind God is only too willing to bestow upon us, and He bestows these gifts upon us by giving us the grace to become as great as any of the saints have ever been.

Yes, "open wide thy mouth," God says to us, "and I will fill it." We open wide our mouths by asking God to make us the saints He wants us to be when He created us out of nothing.

It is to the saints we must go to find what cannot be had in any other class of men, the peace of Christ which surpasses all understanding and not only the peace of Christ but the joy also that is in the Heart of Christ, seeing it is all this the saints possess to a degree greater than any other group of men and women. It is to the saints we must go to get a taste of what the joys of heaven are like, seeing they alone have been given such a taste, it will be given to us too if we walk in their own holy footsteps.

And so, if asked why I became a Catholic, one of the reasons will be given is that it is in the Church of Rome I found the kind of a human being I want to be and that it is in her alone one can get the grace to become as great a saint as anyone who has ever lived. One reason for becoming a Catholic and having the grace to remain one, is because it is in the Church of Rome I found men like St. Augustine as well as all the other intellectual giants who have graced the pages of human history. And so, with all this in view, concerning the great men and women the Church has produced, how can any thinking man and woman help being attracted to her and to want to be what all the saints have been and which same they can only be by having recourse to the means provided by the Church for the attainment of high holiness, the kind the saints alone had attained?

Writing about one's spiritual and intellectual life and which same is what an autobiography really is, is a problem of selection, and this because out of hundreds of incidents, one has to select what is significant in one's own life as well as in the lives of those who would read what one has to say about one's own life. What I mean is something like this. In a way, I was always a Catholic and this because I cannot remember any particular portion of my spiritual and intellectual life during which I failed to be universally minded, and by universally minded, is meant the word Catholic. One cannot speak of Judaism or any other religion of the world in the same term as one does of Catholic Christianity and this because it is only in Christianity the mind and heart of a human being becomes one with the mind and heart of every single human being who was ever been born into this world, Christianity not being racially oriented but universally so, and it is being universally oriented that distinguishes Christianity from every other of the religions we find present in the world today. A Christian is a Christian because and only because he believes in a set of truths handed down by Christ. Christ, who was the most universally-minded human being who ever lived. Christianity teaches us to transcend racial and cultural barriers, and I became Catholic because and only because I wanted to feel and think as does any human being born unto this world, that is to say, in a universal way, Christianity not being for this or that group but for everyone made in the image of God, so to qualify for being a Christian all that is needed is to be created in the image and likeness of God and so it matters not at all into what race or milieu one finds himself born, so that the saying once a Jew always a Jew carries with it no meaning whatever which is of any universal import, and which matters from the angle of the life to come. What matters from the angle of the life to come is whether we accept the truths brought into this world by Him who said, "I am the truth." What matters from the angle of the life to come is whether we accept the tenets of the Christian religion which teach us that the Lord and Creator of the universe took flesh and became as one of us, sin alone excepted. If we accept these truths, we are pleasing in God's eyes, and if we don't accept them, we have to account of our having refused to do so all the time we have found ourselves in our present form of existence. And I, not having been born in a Christian milieu, had to confront this the most serious problem a human being can have in this world, the one the quest for the truth will always be. For, in the eyes of God, we have been put on this earth to get to know what God is like as He stands revealed not only in the pages of the Old Testament alone, but also in the New as well; we just can't close our eyes to the fact that the Incarnation of Christ has taken place, so that as the result of His Incarnation, this world will never be the same again. As a member of the Jewish race, I could not ignore the fact the the Lord and Creator of the universe became a human being, I had to face this fact and reconcile it with the kind of beliefs handed down to me by my Jewish parents: is Christ God or is He not God? If He is God, then how can I avoid the responsibility there is in the search for the truth and accepting that truth when I get the grace to find it, and, thanks be to God, I have found this truth and have done so in the Person of our Lord.

And so, the question of one's conversion to the Catholic religion is really a question of one's search for the whole truth and not for the partial of it which is to be had in the Old Testament writings alone.

I became a Catholic because of reasons I shall never know until I meet God face to face in the next life. I received the grace to be able to believe in all the truths which the Church teaches, and having received such a grace I could not reject it without danger to my immortal soul. In short, whether I wanted to or not, I had to become a Catholic, and because of the grace extended to me by Almighty God, how can one justify refusing to accept grace extended by the Lord and Creator of the universe? Would not such rejection turn out to be a peril to our spiritual and intellectual wellbeing?

And so, when people ask why I became a Catholic, the answer I would like to give is the same a priest gave to someone who asked him why he became a Jesuit. The answer he gave was couched in these words: "Ask the Holy Spirit." I became a Catholic because I was given the grace to do so by Almighty God.

There are so many facets in a person's spiritual and intellectual life that it would be impossible to enter into the details that make up that intellectual and spiritual life, and so there has to be a limit to what can be stated in reference to that spiritual and intellectual life, made up as we said, of so many facets like so many jewels. Our soul is like a jeweled crown composed of the gems of thought we have imbibed in all the books we read dealing with ultimate issues, issues which as rational human beings we have to face and which, to have peace of mind, we can in no wise ignore without peril to our immortal souls.

One of these issues concerns itself with the question of Christ, and so it has to be faced whether one wills or not, seeing that the main reason we have been put on this earth is to seek the truth and to accept that truth no matter where it will lead us. In my case, the quest for the truth led me to the holy Roman Catholic Church and once led to it, there was the moral obligation to accept that truth no matter what the price would be in the acceptance of that truth. For the first three hundred years of Christianity, millions of adherents to that faith paid the full price for that faith and they did so undergoing torture and death. And with this fact before me, the fact of millions of men, women and children having laid down their lives in the defense of their belief in their Catholic faith, am I to cavil at the inconvenience, discomforts and even hatred and ridicule I would encounter in the quest for the truth and in the acceptance of that truth? And, as in the case of other converts to the Catholic Church, I did incur the wrath and hatred and ridicule and even the threat of physical harm and death as the result of my having accepted the grace extended me by Almighty God to become a member of the household of the faith the Church of Rome will always be for those who seek what can be found in her alone, the peace of heart and mind that surpasses all understanding.

As was said in the beginning, the story of one's spiritual and intellectual life is a story of selection, from the thousands of details, we select from that life that which is of relevance to ultimate issues, as well as to the minds and hearts of those who will read what we write. What we have to say has to have about it universal import, so that those reading what we have to say about our own lives should be able to recognize themselves in that life, so that what's important to us and of relevance to us should be important to them as well and to bear relevance to their own spiritual and intellectual outlook so that where this relevance is lacking, there also is lacking what would be of value to others, seeing we do not live for ourselves alone, but we share what is important in our lives and relevant in it with what is important and relevant also in the lives of those who will read what we have to say when we speak of our own selves. Those who read what we have to say about our own selves have to find themselves depicted in what we have to say about our own selves, that is to say, by what we have to say about our own lives, we must bring others into our own lives so as to enable them to share in our own values and to participate in what affords us joy of heart and peace of mind. If we do this, if we have succeeded in enabling others to feel and think as we do, in proportion as we do this, we have succeeded in what we write, and if not, we fail to achieve the goal writing has in view, the goal of enabling others to share in all we ourselves feel to be of importance and relevance.

Those who have already read a portion of this autobiography and whose views along this line I respect, are unanimous that I should continue writing more detailedly the spiritual and intellectual life I have led during the past years. And so, what they suggest has relevance and can't be ignored. I have myself stated that if a person can at all write down his thoughts and feelings for others to read after he is gone, he should by all means do so, seeing we ourselves enjoy reading what others have written, so it is almost an act of charity to oblige those who will come after us with certain important details of our lives for them to enjoy and even be helped by what they read. We both enjoy and are helped by what we read, what those who have lived before us have written, so why should not we make an effort to leave behind for those who will come after us, certain significant details of all we have felt and thought all the time we had been on this earth, seeing this one way of fulfilling the command to love our neighbor as ourselves, we fulfill this commandment by going to the trouble to leave behind a record of our lives for that neighbor to read and enjoy and even being helped by what he reads. And so, with this in view it is hard to stop writing even though the effort to do so entails pain and inconvenience, and we too who write would, with St. Augustine, much rather read what others have written than to write ourselves, seeing that writing of anything worthwhile about ourselves will always remain an arduous task, so arduous, that Joseph Conrad tells us that each morning when he went to his studio to do his daily chore of writing, he was so overcome with the thought of the pain he would go through as the result of that day's writing, that he threw himself on the floor and wept bitter tears because of all he would that day have to go through.

And so, we can see from what has just been said, that writing something worthwhile and which same has substance in it, such writing involves pain of heart and mind seeing what we put down on paper has to be wrested from our inner being, and this wresting from our inner being involves sacrifice and inconvenience and plain hard work. And so, one continues writing about him or herself, all such have to search through their lives to see if they can find in those lives something of relevance for others to read and enjoy doing so, and finding profit to their souls by what they read, have not we ourselves derived both pleasure and profit from what those before us have written concerning their own selves? If we do, how can we avoid the responsibility to leave behind records of our own lives for others to read, can we even for one instance, estimate both the joy and pleasure we have derived from reading what those before us have written? Who is there who can adequately evaluate the joy and profit people have reaped from reading the autobiographies of those who have lived before our own times? What great masterpieces of literature would have been missed if those who write them did not want to go to the trouble and pain entailed in the production of these masterpieces in the form of autobiographies? What treasures would have been lost to the world if St. Augustine did not want to go to the trouble to write his *Confessions*?

And so, with this in view, namely, of all the world would have been deprived by men and women refusing to undergo the pain entailed in writing about their intellectual and spiritual lives, we too, who can at all put down our thoughts and feelings into words, we too have both the responsibility and the obligation of charity to make an effort to put down certain significant factors in our spiritual and intellectual lives for others to read and to enjoy and profit by what they read. And, can we in all justice deny to those who will come after us the favor we have received by reading what those before us did not hesitate to go to the trouble it took for them to put down their thoughts and feelings on paper? And so, with this in view, this writer feels the obligation to continue on in what he began doing a few weeks ago, that is, to search for more facets in his intellectual and spiritual life which can be of help and pleasure for those to read who will be born long after he shall have the blessing entailed in taking leave of this life so that by this taking leave of this life, he can be completely with Christ, completely with Him in the way departure from here can alone make possible. For, as St. Paul so inspiringly declares,

> Therefore, we continue to be confident. We know that while we dwell in the body we are away from the Lord. We walk by faith not by sight. I repeat, we are full of confidence and would much rather be away from the body and be at home with the Lord.
> (2 Cor. 5:6-8)

It is amazing to me, that this beautiful passage is so seldom quoted in books written on the spiritual life. It is amazing that this is so, seeing there is so much joy and profit and consolation to be derived from the reading of these words of the Apostle to the Gentiles and making them our very own by the frequent reading and meditation of them.

As for me, I am tempted to ask this question of myself: Is not all this a long-winded way of stating by what can be said in a few words and in much simpler ones? Cannot we talk about our spiritual and intellectual lives in a way and manner in which it would be easy for others to read? Cannot we simplify the narratives of our spiritual and intellectual lives and state in them only what would be of interest and also pleasurable to read? Must we enter into complicated discussion as to the nature and essence of what we wish to say about ourselves, and is there not a more easy way of our doing so, should we not write about ourselves so that "He who runs may read," to use an expression made famous by the translators of the Old and New Testaments by the compilers of what became known as the King James Version of the Sacred Scriptures!

The answer to this is, we can and we should write in a way and manner for others to enjoy to read, and this in spite of the inconvenience and hardship entailed in our doing so—they say that the writings of Joseph Conrad are among the best, if not the best prose works of the twentieth century. Now, if someone like this author took the trouble entailed in turning out beautiful things to read, why should not we endeavor to do that much for what is of such profit to the soul, namely, to write about the spiritual and intellectual lives we have had the grace to lead to this present day? We both should and can do so, I for one will not be satisfied to write just another story of my conversion to the Church, but one which will be a joy and of profit to read.

When the great English poet John Milton set out to write his masterpiece known as *Paradise Lost*, he began with these words:

> I thence invoke thy aid to my adventurous Song
> That with no *middle* flight intends to soar.
> (Paradise Lost, 10-15)

And, though we can't all be the grandiose authors of great masterpieces like this poem, we can all of us, no matter how poorly gifted in a literary way, write something that would be both a pleasure and of profit to read about our own selves. And so, I too "with no middle flight intend to soar" in an effort to put down certain thoughts and feelings that have been my own for a period of many years, both before and after my conversion from Judaism to the Christian Catholic religion, and to do this it may properly be done with my own limited literary powers. And, though we can't all be Miltons, there are few of us who cannot do all we are able to add to the beauty of God's spiritual world by putting down our own views and experiences so as to help others express their own in whatever manner they best know how, such as by writing and the other arts. If we do this, we will have fulfilled our obligation to love our neighbor as ourselves.

As the result of the Incarnation, God has become Someone not only to be believed in and admired and adored. He is most certainly to be all this to us and infinitely more, the infinitely more we shall get to know in the next life. As the result of His becoming Man, the Lord and Creator of the universe is to be looked upon as our Companion and Friend, for that is what the words "The Lord is my Shepherd" mean and signify in the Hebrew tongue. They in that language mean to point out that of all the dearest things this universe contains, the Lord is the dearest of all, and as such He is not only to be believed in, admired and adored, but He is to be loved as we do the most precious thing that can come up in our lives, and which same, to carry out the first commandment, we should love with our whole heart, with our whole mind and all our strength. We are in this commandment bidden to love the Lord and Creator of the universe as we would love no other thing God has made, be this good and beautiful as it may. We are in the words of the Sacred Scriptures bidden to love God as we would our dearest Friend for a Friend God is and the Companion of our soul as we journey through this vale of tears. Yes, the Lord is indeed our Shepherd and this because the Lord is indeed our Friend, has He not more than once been referred to as the "Friend of friends"? As the result of His becoming Man, the Lord and Creator of the universe is no longer Someone afar off, some sort of concept and abstract Reality; the Lord and Creator of the universe has become one of us, sin alone excepted, so that we may in that way be near and dear to Him and that we may in that way love Him as we do our own selves and those with whom we are brought together into intimate relationship. The God which as the close followers of our divine Lord we have the grace to be, this Great and Good and Beautiful Lord, is no longer the far-off Being described in the Old Testament writings. He has now become our close Companion and Friend whom we may in a mystical way, see and hear and taste and touch, and it is this Great, Good and Beautiful Lord who once walked this earth, which I as Jewish convert have the blessing and grace to not only believe in but to love as I do no other things God has made be that good and beautiful as it may, "Love," St. Augustine says, "that which God has not made?"

And so, as we think of all this, as we call to mind the great and ineffable mystery of God's becoming Man, we should be grateful for the fact that we have been given the grace to be the close companions of Christ the Lord, and how sorry we should feel for all those who, for reasons known only to God, are deprived of such a grace, how we shall for all eternity revel in the thought that we have been given the grace to become the blessed members of the household of the true faith the Church of Rome will always continue to be! How we shall for all eternity thank God for giving us the grace to enable us to believe in the truths the Church teaches and the peace of soul such belief brings with it, as well as the joy of heart and mind induced by the belief that it is in the Church of Rome we find "rest for the mind and peace for the heart," to use an expression of Fredrick Ozanam, who is about to be raised up to the altars of the Church he loved with such a vast amount of intensity and passionateness.

I shall for all eternity thank God for giving me the grace to become a Catholic and consider that grace as the greatest favor God can bestow upon anyone who finds himself or herself outside the true Church. "You have led me to a happiness which admits of no description," are the words of St. Elizabeth Seton written to the person directly responsible for her becoming a Catholic, and I too have been led to the same kind of happiness which admits of no description. When the greatest Jewish convert the Church has so far produced, the Ven. Mary Paul Libermann used to get discouraged he kept repeating these words to himself: "I am a Christian, I am a Christian," realizing there can be no greater source of happiness than in receiving the grace to become a member of the household of the faith the Church of Rome can alone be for a human being, she it is who will always constitute the gate of heaven for a human being, there being no other path on which to trod to Paradise.

And so, when I think of all this, when I call to mind all God has done for me giving me the grace to become a Catholic, I am besides myself with joy of heart and mind and one reason for my desire to get to heaven is that it is only in the next life I will be able to adequately thank God for the gift of my holy Catholic religion, a religion the possession of which brings with it the glory of ten thousand worlds and the riches that all these worlds contain. Many years ago, one of the priests I lived with here at Xavier, said these words to me: "How's things, Charlie," and the answer I gave was contained in these words: "I am a Catholic; I can't complain."

Now as I look back at these words I am struck with the profundity they contain, seeing when a person receives the gift of being able to believe in the only true Church, he is the recipient of what God Himself is unable to surpass in bestowing upon that person, seeing he is the blessed recipient of a gift which will constitute for him or her a source of unending joy and delight. Such a person will for all eternity receive the blessings that come with being a Catholic.

Well, this subject of being a Catholic is so vast and immense it can never be written enough about, so no matter how much we may say along this line, we cannot do suffcent justice to it. With this in view, I shall now stop for a while before asking for the grace to continue with the story of my spiritual and intellectual journey through the world of time.

Here I am again, finding myself confronted with the problem as to what I shall do regarding the matter of the rest of the autobiography, and whether I should pray to God to know what to do in order to continue on writing it, or whether it may be God's will not to go any further along this line. But time and prayer will tell, because it is a most momentous thing to put down on paper all that happens to us as we proceed on our way from the present life to the one to come, and for which reason the Jews of old were called Hebrews, the word Hebrew being derived from the root which means to pass over and to pass on. The Jews of old were called Hebrews because they were the passers-over from time to eternity, and from this life to the one to come, and in this sense every Catholic is a Hebrew, because every Catholic is meant by God to pass on from this life to the one to come.

And so, as I find myself moving along on my passage-way from time to eternity, I begin to reflect on everything I have already passed through during the eighty-five years of my existence in time. As I do so, I ask God for the grace to recall all the important events in my life which have a direct bearing on the way I have the grace to now think and feel, namely, in a way that's supernatural and not limited to aspects that are merely temporal. As I find myself proceeding along the path of time, I ask myself this question: How and by what means have I had the grace to have arrived at the present way I now feel and think, and which way is the one all the saints have trodden. Along this line, does not the prophet Isaiah say to us the following words: "A highway will be there, called the holy way" (Is. 35:8). I have always taken these words to signify that in order to get to heaven we must proceed there on the same way on which He Himself passed on to His Father in heaven and which same way is the way of the Cross. And so, as I find myself reflecting on all that I have already gone through, and wonder how I got to where I now am, as I do so, I realize that it is all due to God's goodness to me and it is to Him I owe the blessing of having the grace to be a member of the only true Church and which same the Church of Rome can alone be for a believing and reasonable human being. And, as we once said, though there are other religions in the world, and they have all of them certain of God's truths, in none of them can one find the fullness of this truth, seeing it is in her alone, the Church founded by Christ nineteen hundred years ago, that the fullness of all God wants us to both have and possess can be had. I think of this every time I call to mind God's goodness to me in giving me the grace to be able to believe all that the Church teaches and which same it is God's express will I should believe, seeing it is by means of this belief that rest is to be had by the heart and peace by the mind. It is in the Church alone we find all that the heart yearns for and for which the mind of man can never cease pining and longing.

> My soul yearns and pines [Hebrew, faints]
> for the courts of the Lord—
> My heart and my flesh
> cry out for the living God.
> (Ps. 84:3)

How perfectly the psalmist here expresses the longing in the human heart and mind for what has to be in that heart and in that mind to be what in the eyes of God a human being is meant to be.

It most certainly is a grace from God to be able to express in words all that went on in my heart and mind all the time I began to think and reason about everything with which I came into contact since I have from my earliest youth wondered as to what God would have me do, why I was born, and what will happen to us after we depart from this life, and it took exactly fifty-two years to receive an answer to the questions that presented themselves to my mind ever since I am able to remember. The answer that came to me to the questions that presented themselves to my reasoning self has been given me by the holy Roman Catholic Church, since in her alone can be had an answer to the questions that come up in this life, the questions relating as to the meaning of our existence in time, and as regards everything God would have us do to have a happy life after the one we are now in will be blessedly over.

I heard of a story told of John Moody, the founder of the *Wall*

Street Journal. He and his wife with their twenty-one year old son, were vacationing in Italy. While there, their son died. After the body had been lowered in the grave, the grief-stricken father said these words to the Episcopalian minister who was presiding at the grave: "Is that all there is to it?" The answer he received was expressed in these words: "I don't know." Mr Moody left the cemetery with this determination. He wanted an answer which was yes or no. He found the answer was yes, there is another life and as the result of this answer be became a Catholic.

Like so many distraught and confused souls, I too wanted to know if there is an answer to the questions a human being can ask and found there is such an answer and that it is to be had in the Church of Rome for she alone can categorically state that there exists another life after this one is over, and that when we die, we go to the place of everlasting rest the name Paradise signifies—we do not die if we are Catholics. If we are Catholics we enter into the kind of life into which they have gone who had the grace to be able to believe in all of the truths the Church of Rome has been commissioned to teach by Almighty God in the Person of His Son. It is these truths I got the grace to embrace and believe in when I became a Catholic and which same truths answered all the questions a human being is capable of asking all the time he stays on this earth. It is about these answers to the questions that presented themselves to my mind I would like to refer as I go on writing this biography, for it would give joy to the hearts and minds of those who read concerning these answers, and how consoling it is to have them clarified and brought out in so satisfying a way as the Church has the grace to do. Does not the psalmist say: "On waking, I shall be content in your presence" (Ps. 17:15) and which words have reference to the resurrection from the dead.

Setting out to write the story of one's life is like setting out on the high seas in a lifeboat—there are such a vast number of incidents in that life from which one has to choose, that it bewilders the mind in an effort to decide which of these incidents to note down by way of remembrances, and which of them would be of no relevance to the reader of that life, and which same would only serve to confuse those who would make an effort to understand what the author of that life is trying to make clear and comprehensible. It is no more easy to write the story of one's spiritual and intellectual life than it would be to try to cross the ocean in the lifeboat that has been mentioned. With this in view, the difficulty entailed in such a task, one can readily understand the diffidence with which one takes up his pen to write the story of his life. One hesitates doing so on account of the bewildering number of the details connected with such a life and the utter inability to deal with each of the incidents and circumstances that go to the making of a human existence, so it is for this reason that the analogy of the lifeboat in which one sets out to cross the ocean is so apt in this case, and so relevant. It fits the picture perfectly. And, just as we would hesitate crossing the ocean in a lifeboat, so do we in the same way hesitate to put down on paper all we have gone through in the course of a lifetime, there being too many factors connected with such a lifetime to attempt to enumerate even a small number of these factors. Still, as was stated in an earlier part of this narrative, one has the obligation of charity to those who will come after us, to leave a record of God's goodness to us all the time we found ourselves in the present form of this existence.

And so, we go on with the effort to state what should be stated and we do so with the hope that God will assist us in such an effort, the effort to leave behind a record of all of God's goodness to us all the time we stayed in this life. In this respect, we proceed with the hope that just as we enjoy to read of the lives of those who have lived before we were born, so do we in the same way hope that after we die, those who will come after us, that they too will enjoy reading about the lives we have led, and do so with profit by what they read. Also, as we have said, this effort on our part to leave behind a written account of the lives we lived, may even entail an obligation of charity, seeing that in being commanded to love our neighbor, leaving behind a record of our lives may really be a form of charity to them. For just as we enjoy reading about the lives of those who preceded us, so those who will be born after our departure from this life, they too will enjoy reading about the life we have ourselves gone through. And so, maybe the command to love our neighbor consists in the effort we make to leave behind a record of our lives for them to enjoy and profit from such a record.

Recently, I read these words about St. Vincent de Paul: "He could not read his own writing with out tears when he thought that the passages from his pen did not proceed from his own mind but from the God of all goodness." As I read these words, this is the thought that came to me: Would it be presumptuous for someone else besides St. Vincent to feel and think that the thoughts that came from his pen "proceeded not from his own mind but from the God of all goodness"? Would it be presumptuous to feel that what God did for all His saints He is both ready and willing to do for us as well? He Himself says to each of us, "Open wide your mouth, and I will fill it" (Ps. 81:11).

It is definitely the devil's aim to keep good men and women from becoming saints, we said good men and women, because the devil does not mind our being ordinary good Catholics. What he dreads is that we aim and reach for the summit of perfection, which being a saint is. Along this line, does not Fredrick Ozanam say the following: "Ordinary Catholics are plentiful enough: we need saints." Then we have the words of St. Vincent de Paul himself stating that "when God wishes to bring forth great events in the Christian world, he begins by sowing the seed of saints." And, what is it that the holy psalmist makes his complaint of? Does he not say, "Woe is me, there are no longer any saints on this earth," and by saints he here designates godlike human beings who ask for the grace to give themselves completely to Christ. It is the one hundred percent Christians God has in view and which He calls by the name of "friends."

This subject is a most lengthy one, seeing by it is involved the whole history of the Catholic Church, seeing that the history of the holy Roman Apostolic Church is nought else but the history of the saints of God, she alone being capable of producing men and women and even children who give themselves completely up to love for Christ and withhold not one iota of their being from this love of Him.

I personally, since my entrance into the Church, have always felt that it is being a saint that matters, this, and no other thing.

For, as a convert, I could see no good reason for becoming a Catholic and not at the same time to ask God to make me one of His saints. Why, I said to myself, should anyone go through all the trials and inconveniences and even threats of physical harm and even death, as is the case in some people becoming Catholics; why should anyone go through all he has to to embrace the only true faith and be willing and content to be just another good Catholic? Does not our Lord say we "should launch out into the deep" and by "deep" is not meant mere water, but the depths of doctrine. It is into the depths of all the Church teaches we should ask God for the grace to penetrate into, and which same cannot be done save by means of the Cross as St. John of the Cross makes so clear and evident in the following words:

> For the soul cannot enter these caverns or reach these treasures if, as we said, she does not first pass to the divine wisdom through the straits of exterior and interior suffering. For one cannot reach in this life what is attainable of these mysteries of Christ without having suffered much, and without having received numerous intellectual and sensible favors from God, and without having undergone much spiritual activity (Spiritual Canticle, Stanza 37:4).

In writing along this line one has to be careful to adhere to the object for which he first set out to write, which in this case is the story of the soul's journey to God by means of a person becoming a Catholic. For what is it to become a Catholic but to set out on the road which will lead that person to the paradisal joys they experience who are now in heaven and I, personally, became a Catholic so that I may in that way have the grace to know in this life, get a taste of what the joys of heaven are like, and most certainly receive a taste of these joys by getting the grace to be able to believe in all that the Church teaches as regards our moral and spiritual and intellectual life. And just as St. John of the Cross teaches, we "cannot reach in this life what is attainable of these mysteries of Christ without having suffered much," etc. It is to be enabled to enter into the thickets of the mysteries of Christ we become Catholics, and for that purpose only. We become Catholics because we get the grace to perceive that it is only by being a member of the household of the true Faith the Church of Rome will always be, that we will receive whatever we have to have to become the close followers of our divine Lord.

Referring to what we have to have to attain the goal for which we have been put on this earth, the prophet Isaiah has this to say:

A highway will be there,
called the holy way;
No one unclean may pass over it.
(Is. 35:8)

Ever since I entered the Church, I have always wanted to believe that the "highway" and the "holy way" of which the prophet here speaks, is the holy Roman Apostolic Catholic Church and it is She alone who is thus designated, seeing it is on the road She can alone be for a human being, that it is God's will we should proceed to our eternal reward Christ shall be for us after this brief and painful existence will be over in our case.

And so, as one gets the grace to recall the events and incidents of one's life, one cannot help being filled with gratitude to God for His having watched over and exercised His merciful providence over him. And seeing one cannot thank God enough for the favors he or she has already received, the desire that comes over such a person, is to look forward to where such gratitude may be adequately expressed in the next life. Is it not for this very reason we find the psalmist saying, "Lead me forth from prison, that I may give thanks to your name" (Ps. 142:8)?

Something in myself tells me I must hurry up and finish this autobiography, though in reality there cannot be a finish to all that should be stated which would be a source of satisfaction to the reader and to the one who does the writing. And so, when I think of the lifeboat adrift on a vast ocean of water and of the person in the lifeboat, it strikes me as an excellent figure to describe the effort to put on paper all that went on in my heart and since the first day I was in the Church, the days before that day, not really being of any importance because I felt I began to really live after having had the waters of baptism poured on my head, the results of which giving me the grace to look at all things from the point of view of the life to come and not from the limited perspective of time alone. Along this line, I like to think of what St. Francis de Sales said of his namesake, St. Francis of Assisi: "God gave to St. Francis a view of the whole world as a miracle of love." And, though I know I shall myself never be worthy of such a sublime view of the world I am in, I don't think there is another way of describing the outlook on all things I have had the grace to have since I became a Catholic, since with that faith, there has come a vision of things no longer limited to time alone but embracing the view they have of what's important in the life of a human being who are now in heaven, something the Catholic outlook can alone bestow on the mind and heart of a human being, and which same has been so beautifully expressed in the words of St. Stanislaus Kotska, S.J.: "I was not born for this world but for the next, and for the next, and not for this world I will live." I had the grace to come upon these words as soon as I entered the Church, and as soon as I read them, I determined to make these words my very own, and that I too was not born for this world but for the next, and so not for this world but for the next I will live. Is it not a sad thing that so few dispose themselves for the graces God is so ready and so willing to give us to become saints, seeing all we have to do to become saints is not to live for this world, but for the next. Along this line does not St. Francis de Sales say to us that "we don't think enough of eternity"? Even long before I ever became a Catholic, I felt that we were too time-conscious and that much of the misery we experience in this ilfe is due to the fact that we don't think enough of the life to come and that we are not eternity-minded enough. Also, did not the greatest enemy Christianity ever had, Friedrich Nietzsche say: *"Ich liebe dich oh Ewigkeit"* (I love thee, oh eternity). Now, if someone as unhappy as he was, could say these words how much more should not we who are blessed with the only true faith, say the same thing? We ought to be ashamed of ourselves not being able to do so, seeing the love and graces God has in His goodness bestowed upon us by giving us what so many good and holy people outside the Church have not been bestowed on, the grace to have the other world in view.

To quote again the words of this remarkable Jesuit saint who died only after a few years in this life, we have all of us not been born for this world, but for the next and so not for this world but for the next we should live, something we will have the grace to do if we ask for the grace by which alone can be done, we cannot live for the next life if we do not embrace the only faith that can enable us to do so, and in order to become saints, we have to have the other life in view and not this one alone. And where, one may ask, can one find saints outside the holy Roman Catholic Church? Where, in what religion can we find a St. Augustine, a St. Thomas Aquinas, a St. Bernard, a St. Teresa, a St. John of the Cross and so many others who equal these in their love for the Love in essence Christ can alone be for a human being. I became a Catholic because it is in her alone we can attain the goal of our heart's desire Jesus in the state of glory is.

I know I said this before. But this thought is so beautiful and so necessary it cannot be repeated enough. We cannot repeat enough that it is only in the Church of Rome the full riches of the Godhead may be had and this because, the Church of Rome being Christ Himself, the full riches of the Godhead dwells in Her, seeing the fullness of the Godhead is embodied in the Person of our Lord. So it is to the Church of Rome we must go for the fullness of what we have, to have rest for the mind and peace for the heart, and this even as one of the greatest Catholic layman once said, and which words are worth quoting over and over. "I die," this saintly person says, "in the holy Catholic, Apostolic and Roman Church. I have known the difficulties of belief of the present age, but my whole life has convinced me that there is neither rest for the mind nor peace for the heart save in the Church and in obedience to her authority" (Fredrick Ozanam). Let those, who for one reason or another seriously think of leaving the Church, take these words to heart before taking the fatal step. Let those who look for a home for their soul and who want rest for the mind and peace for the heart, go to where alone this rest and this peace may be had on this earth. Let them turn to no other religion for such rest and for such peace, seeing that such rest and such peace is meant by God to be had in Her alone whose Mystical Body She will always be. It is only in the Church of Rome that that may be had for which we have been put on this earth, in Her and nowhere else, and it is for this reason the Church of Rome will always attract to Herself hearts and minds on which rests the blessing of Almighty God. It is to the Church of Rome we must go for what is meant by God to be had nowhere else, and a convert realizes this as soon as he or she gets the grace to take this Church to his or her heart, and looks upon Her as the Bride of Christ, to which the soul of every human being is meant to be mystically wedded. To repeat, it is to Rome we must go to have what has to be had to live in this world with a certain amount of peace and happiness, seeing it is in Her alone this peace and this happiness is meant by God to be had. It is meant to be had nowhere else and in no other thing God has made, be this good and beautiful as it may.

I know, without having anyone telling me, what a worthwhile thing it is to write an autobiography of my life, still, it is not an easy matter to accomplish, and this on account of the numerous details the life of a human being entails, and especially the life of someone who has had the blessing to become a member of the only true Church the Roman, Apostolic and Catholic Church will always be for a believing human being and one who is endowed by God with the truth promulgated by Her. And while it is not a too difficult thing to record the details of a life devoid of the kind of grace one received by becoming a Catholic, it is a thousand times more so when one has been endowed by God with the gift of faith in the only true Church, seeing that such faith fills the soul of that person with ten thousand blessings too numerous to retell and to record in the limited space of a biography. We read in the psalms and often do so, that we should "exult in the Lord" and in the Hebrew this means we should *shout* for joy at the realization that we are loved by God and that He loves us, and if we are bidden to exult in the Lord on account of the love we have the grace to have for God, how additional should our exultation be at the realization of our having the grace to be the blessed members of the only true Church, the Church of Rome is? As far as I am concerned, I can never exult enough for having received the grace to become a Catholic, and when I will pass on from this life to the next, this exultation will continue on and it will do so in the ineffable way in which all things in the next life will be accomplished, seeing we will in the next life see and hear and feel and taste in a wondrous and ineffable way all that we now experience in an imperfect one. It is in heaven alone we will be able to fully appreciate the grace we have received to become the blessed members of God's true Church, the Church for which millions upon millions have had the grace to lay down their lives—is there, has there ever been, a religion that has produced so many martyrs as did the holy Roman Catholic Church? What religion has had such a vast number of men, women and children lay down their lives in the defense of its teaching as did the Church of Rome? And this factor alone, that of the millions upon millions who received the grace to lay down their lives in defense of the truths of the faith, is sufficient to make one wonder if the religion in which he or she believes which is not the holy Roman Catholic one, is the religion God wants these people to have and hold on to and embrace, seeing it is in the Church alone the whole of God's truths may be had, in Her and in no other religious persuasion.

It is to the Church we must go for the peace of heart and rest of the mind we have to have to bear the troubles of this life, seeing without this peace and without this rest, it is practically impossible to live a normal intellectual and spiritual life. Yes, I am carried away by love for the holy Roman Apostolic Catholic Church and I am not in the least averse in saying so, seeing if we are to take pride in and glory in anything God has made, should we not take pride in the glory our Lord Himself is! Along this line did not our Lord find fault with those about Him who gloried in each other and were therefore deprived of the grace to glory in His Heavenly Father?

It is God's holy will we should take a holy kind of pride in the fact that we have been given the grace to become the blessed members of the household of the only true faith the Church will always be for an enlightened human being, enlightened by the grace of God and which light can alone illuminate our deep interior being, the deep interior being which alone matters in the life of a human being, and which same God has promised to protect and safeguard. "I am a Catholic; I can't complain," were the words with which I replied to the question as to how things are with me. I did this, because of the realization that compared with the gift of faith I received fifty-two years ago, what are all things I fail to have? Is there anything God can give us apart and outside of this faith which will in any way compare with that gift? There is not; so it is for this reason that in answer as to how things are with me, I said: "I am a Catholic; I can't complain."

The problem of writing about the interior life is that we have to use the same words with which we talk about the exterior life. And the same thing is true when we speak about our conversion, seeing that what's converted is our inner being, the outer one remaining the same as it was prior to the transformation of our soul in Christ, for that is what a conversion is. It is the transformation of our inner being, and not the outer one. The outer part of our being will remain what it is until its dissolution by death, for it is the soul that counts and it is the soul that's converted to God, so as to live the Life Christ has to be for a human being if the human being is at all to live the kind of spiritual and intellectual life we are meant by God to live....

There used to be a saying that "he who does not have the Church for his Mother cannot have God for his Father," so I wonder what has in the course of the Christian centuries become of these words, and why we do not hear them quoted nowadays, when the need for them has never been greater. Today, more than ever in the times gone by, we need the kind of spiritual and intellectual guide the Church of Rome is, seeing as history rolls on, so do the many errors and aberrations roll on with Her. We are living in one of the most disturbing ages in the history of the Christian world, so there is need for the kind of spiritual and intellectual guide the Church of Rome is. We have need of an institution the Church of Rome is and one which is itself guided by the Holy Spirit, seeing it is the Holy Spirit that guides us by means of the Church and that Holy Spirit resides in Her alone.

I will be with you all days, our Lord said to the Church of Rome, thus guaranteeing Her divine guidance. To what other religion has our Lord spoken words like these? To what other religion has our Lord said: "I for my part declare to you, you are Rock and on this rock I will build my church, and the jaws of death shall not prevail against it" (Mt. 16:18). It is to the Church of Rome these words have reference and so we should rest in peace when we see Her attacked on all sides, and this both by those within and without. There will never come a time when the holy Roman Catholic Church will not have enemies with whom She will have to wage unending warfare. For, just as Christ was hated so will the Bride the Church of Rome is, be hated with Him. We are passing through a period in the history of the world in which the Church of Rome is the most hated institution on this earth, and all this hatred of Her proceeds from the enemy of the human race the devil will always be. It is he, Satan, who reviles everything sacred, he it is who will always be the bitter enemy of all that is sublime and which same will always be safeguarded by the Church of Rome. Who is it, we may ask, that stands up for the supernatural and the divine? Who holds up to us the hope of heaven's joys? Where, in what institution do we hear these joys spoken of? What religion is there which is so suffused with the divine element as the one established by Christ? Where can we go for the mysteries to be had in the Church of Rome? Where are the supernatural realities present in today's world?

We cannot have God for a Father if we do not have the Church for our Mother, the Mother of our spiritual and intellectual life. Is it not She who guards and protects that spiritual and intellectual life? From how many false philosophies has She not already set us free, and from how many falsehoods and errors? It is to the Church of Rome we have to go for the truths Christ came to bring by means of His Incarnation, truths concerning the nature and essence of the Godhead. "I am that I am," our Lord says to us by the mouth of Moses, and He in these words indicates the eternity of His Being. I am Eternal Being, Christ says to us, and the Church of Rome repeats these words with Him, He, Christ and the Church constituting one Person. Christ is the Church, and the Church is Christ; where one exists, the other is also present and this in an ineffable and mystical way.

Do we want Truth, do we want Beauty in essence and nature? We will find this Truth and this Beauty where alone it is meant by God to be.

> Ah, you are beautiful, my beloved...
> Ah, you are beautiful, my lover, yes you are lovely.
> (Song of Songs, 1:15-16)

It is regarding the Bride of Christ the Church is these words have been spoken, She it is who is the Beautiful one in whom there can be nothing out of harmony with all that's of a purely celestial nature. Besides, aren't we told that we should "Sing to the Lord a new Song," the new Song Christ can alone be for a human being and which same Song every convert sings when he gets the grace to become a member of the only true Church founded by Him?

Conversion to the true Faith is the Song God puts into the mouths of all those who have the grace to become the transformed and enraptured human beings who have by means of their conversion become transfigured in Christ the Lord, so that as the result of their thus being transfigured, they are no longer what they had been prior to their conversion, seeing a mystical transformation has taken place in their inmost self, which is expressed by the Hebrew terms for "heart." For it is the "heart" that's been converted, that inmost self of that person and not the exterior portion of his or her being, which will be dissolved by death. It is the inmost self we take with us on our way out of this world, seeing there is nothing in that inmost self which is under the jurisdiction of the laws of time and decay, there being that in a human being death cannot touch, and which same is protected by God, overseen and cared for by Him as His most cherished possession. "We are souls, not bodies, " St. Ambrose says to us, the bodies he says, are our clothing.

And so, as we find ourselves brought into the household of the only true Church, we exult and rejoice to find ourselves at home with God, and not only at home with Him but we find ourselves mystically fused with and identified with His own Beauteous Self, seeing it is to Him, to Christ, we address the words, "Ah, you are beautiful, my lover, yes, you are lovely." Now Christ being one Person with the Church, what we say to Him we say to Her whose Bride the Church of Rome will always be for those who do what they are able to dispose themselves for the graces of conversion.

In a way, there is no purpose and no plan to this story because the ways of God are purposeless seeing they are infinite in extent and so they cannot be comprehended by the human mind. When God takes us by the hand, as He does when we are led by Him by being able to believe in all that has been revealed to us by the deposit of the faith, we do not perceive the method by which

God's grace takes root in the depth of our inner being, something goes on in that depth which we shall only fully understand when we get to heaven. On earth, the ways by which we are led to the household of the only true faith are too ineffable and too mysterious to be able to be understood. All we know is that by means of His grace, God has worked a transformation in our souls so that after this transformation we cannot recognize what we had been prior to our conversion. We are conscious of a change that has taken place in our thinking and feeling; but what exactly that change is, we are unable to say in words of any kind. It is the grace of God working in the soul that produces such a change, and being grace how can it be understood by the human mind? All we do know is that something has occurred within ourselves, which we cannot express in a clear-cut way and that, though we are the same people we have been prior to our conversion, in a mystical way, we are other than what we have been.

In a very remarkable passage St. John of the Cross makes reference to this transformation of the soul in Christ, which is produced by means of God's grace, and here is what this Doctor of mystical theology has to say in reference to what certain converts experience as the result of their conversion:

> This night withdraws the spirit from its customary manner of experience to bring it to the divine experience which is foreign to every human way. It seems to the soul in this night that it is being carried out of itself by afflictions. At other times a man wonders if he is not being charmed, and goes about with wonderment over what he sees and hears. Everything seems so very strange even though he is the same as always. The reason is that he is being made a stranger to his usual knowledge and experience of things so that thus annihilated in this respect, he may be informed with the divine, which belongs more to the next life than to this.
> (*Dark Night of the Soul*, Bk 2, Ch.9)

And while it remains true that these words of St. John of the Cross have reference to the mystical graces of infused prayer, every conversion has in itself a certain similarity to what he says, because in every conversion there takes place a transformation in the ways of thinking and feeling, so that as the result of this transformation, a person can hardly recognize the self he or she had been prior to this transformation that conversion brings about. And so what takes place in the mystical state occurs also to a limited degree in the life of a convert, from the wrong to the right way of looking at things and which same are nature. The supernatural convert is also a little disconcerted by what has taken place in his inmost self, so he is kind of taken aback by the realization he is no longer what he had been prior to his conversion, this experience resembling that of the one receiving mystical graces of infused prayer and infused contemplation.

I realize only too well how far astray I have gone from the intent I had when I started out writing this autobiography. But there is no such thing as a competely mystical life, and a completely non-mystical one, seeing every human being, by virtue of his being made in the image of God, has about him that which cannot be comprehended in the present life, that is to say, a divine quality which is the result of this being made in God's image. We sense this divine quality when we get the grace to become Catholics.

When someone asked Momson, who had written a fifteen-volume history of the Roman Empire, who was going to read all those volumes, he replied that he did not care if anyone was going to read them and that he had written them for himself. The same is true of all the great masterpieces; they were created primarily to give satisfaction to the author who created them and secondarily for the pleasure and satisfaction of those who are going to read them. I am sure if John Milton was asked why he had composed *Paradise Lost,* he would have said that he did so for the need of his own soul, the need that soul of his had for poetic beauty. The same is true of those who have written biographies of their own spiritual and intellectual lives. These have done so for the need they felt to give utterance to the feelings they had to record the beautiful and holy incidents of their lives, as to, by means of these utterances, give glory to God. They did so because of the conviction they had that there is in the life of every human being something beautiful and worthwhile, so that if that human can at all do so, he should ask God for the grace to put down on paper whatever beautiful and holy thoughts he is able to remember, and this primarily for his own need and satisfaction. If others will read what that person has to say, all well and good. But it is not for others but for themselves writers have written about themselves. They have done so for the need they had to look back at the years they had spent on this earth, so as to in that way record for themselves all the beautiful and sublime incidents and moments in their lives. They did so to re-live the holy and joyous times they had experienced so as to in that way thank God for these joyous times and these holy and sublime experiences.

The present author asks God for the grace to do the same thing. He too, in order to glorify our divine Lord and to show gratitude to Him for all the gifts of body and mind he had all his life received from Him, he too, feels the need to recall some of the moments and incidents of his life, so he may in that way receive the grace to sort of re-live these moments and these incidents, so he may in that way give glory to God for His having enabled him to experience all he did on his way from this life to the next. And so, with this holy purpose, that of giving glory to God, we ask for the grace to continue doing what we set out in all that has already been written, which in this case is to give thanks to God for the grace to have become a member of the Church of Rome, and by means of the graces he receives from this membership to attain not merely the salvation of his immortal soul, but also the sanctification of that soul. It would have been to no purpose for that person to have been born, if he had not received the grace to be re-born in Him who will for all eternity constitute our All. So that possessing Him, we shall be the blessed possessors of everything we have to have to be happy not only in this life alone but also for that other and infinitely more beautiful one, in the one to come. It is for that life we are being prepared by means of our holy Catholic faith, seeing that if we have the Church for our Mother we are guaranteed to have God for our Father.

There are so many needs we have in this life, that unless we are the blessed members of the only true Church, they can in no way be completely satisfied, these needs being of a moral, spiritual and intellectual nature, and the Church of Rome being the Mother of these needs, She alone is meant by God to satisfy these needs, the ones infused by God in the depths of the soul's substance. And, we have needs that are both ordinary and extraordinary, seeing for an enlightened human being, both these needs are equally necessary. We have need for someone to guide us in the ordinary ways of our prayer lives, and also in the extraordinary ones, if and when it pleases God to lead us into these ways, and proceed on them to Himself. "I am the way," our Lord says to us indicating it is on the path He had Himself trodden we must walk to eternal happiness, and sometimes these ways are ordinary and other times they're extraordinary, and if the latter, we have need for the divine guidance on these ways the Church of Christ is meant to be.

How many there are who are the recipients of genuine mystical graces, but they have no one to guide them on the road it is God's will they should proceed on to Himself? There are a whole host of men and women, who, had they had the gift of the faith in the true Church, they would have had someone to guide them on their road to the paradisal bliss, the extraordinary graces instilled into the substance of the soul. All such, to develop along deeply mystical lines, and to avoid the pitfalls such a life entails, have need for a St. John of the Cross and a Teresa of Avila to guide and instruct them in the ways of mystical graces. But, where outside the Church of Rome, are we to find those with the skill and experiences, and the graces of a St. John of the Cross and a St. Teresa of Avila? What other religion has produced such spiritual and intellectual giants as She has had the grace to give birth to? Where, in what religion outside the one the Church of Rome is, will we find a St. Bernard and others like him, equipped with what they have to have who will lead others along the paths of mystical graces, seeing that these paths are filled with so many dangers, so that those outside the Church cannot proceed on them without risks to themselves. What religion has given birth to the great mystics of the Church of Rome? Can we find in these religions a St. Gregory the Great, a St. Augustine, a St. Francis of Assisi, a St. Catherine of Siena? I know only too well this has already been stated but being of the importance it is, it cannot be re-stated often enough. Why don't we more often refer to the spiritual and intellectual advantage to be had in the Church of Rome? Is it for this very reason she will continue attracting to herself the minds and hearts of men like St. Augustine and Cardinal Newman?

When they see the spiritual and intellectual treasures the Church of Rome contains, when they learn about the nature of these treasures, men and women cease to be satisfied with the religions they are in, and so they get the grace to become Catholics. The writer of these words has done so himself, when he got the grace to perceive the spiritual and intellectual superiority Christianity had over the religion in which he was brought up. And, what this author has had the grace to experience, others outside the Church of Rome also have the grace to experience.

As long as this world shall last there will always be men and women of noble mentalities who will be possessed by the need for the fullness of the faith to be had in the Church of Rome. And so, in spite of the inconveniences such people will experience and great sacrifices, there will always be those who will feel the need for the fullness of the truths brought into this world by God's becoming Man, and endowing the Church with the fullness of Himself. It is in Her, as in our Lord Himself, in whom the fullness of the Godhead dwells bodily, She being but another name for our divine Lord. She it is, in which the fullness of the truth will always exist so that it can be had by Her alone.

Yes, I do repeat myself. But how is anyone to speak of divine things without risking this kind of repetition? Do we say the Hail Mary too many times? And, do not these words sound sweeter to us the more often they are spoken? "Holy, holy, holy is the Lord of hosts?" Who will accuse the prophet Isaiah of being repetitious by saying the word "holy" three times? When we love someone we cannot say we love him enough, since the more often we say we love him the more often does that person experience delight in hearing us say he is being loved. To emphasize the importance of what is stated, we find the Holy Scriptures repeating the same thought over and over, this being especially the case in the book of the Psalms in which we find the same thoughts repeated in parallel columns. Enough said for one day, so I'll sign off.

*   *   *

The ship, this autobiography, has been standing still awhile, so it is time for it to move on gliding along the vast ocean of events and incidents that have long since passed into oblivion; we have to move on in this life where to stand still is to die. We have to move on in this vast sea of mysteries to the greatest Mystery of all, which the Most Holy Trinity is for a believing human being. In the words of the poet, we have to move on towards that

> One far-off divine event,
> To which the whole creation moves.
> (*In Memoriam* Tennyson)

And although these words are not specifically Christian and Catholic, they can be made so by stating that that "far-off Divine event" is the State of Glory and the Beatific Vision in which we shall see God face-to-face, and this even as His great prophet Moses had the grace to see the Lord and Creator and Holy Redeemer of the universe, namely, our divine Lord, whom, when we shall see in the state of glory, we shall say

> Ah, you are beautiful, my beloved...
> Ah, you are beautiful, my lover—yes
> you are lovely.
> (Song of Songs, 1:15-16)

We shall continue saying these words to the Bridegroom of our soul and we shall do so for all eternity. We shall for all eternity say to God how beautiful He is in His divine Son, and how beautiful they are who have the grace to be with Him in the state of glory.

It is getting to the point that instead of writing down the story of my spiritual and intellectual life, what I'll end up doing is to write a poem in the words of prose, the poem every true life is as the author of the *Religio Medici* says it is in the words: "Now for my life. It is a miracle of thirty years, which to relate, were not a history, but a piece of poetry, and would sound to common ears like a fable" (*Religio Medici*, Sect. 12, by Sir Thomas Browne, M.D.). One can often think of these words, and this in connection with his or her own life, since looked at from the angle of things divine, the whole world is nothing but some vast poetic masterpiece. It is the "miracle of love," the vision of the miracle of love which God had shown to St. Francis of Assisi. And so, as I myself look back on my life I can readily sympathize with the words of Sir Thomas Browne and thank him for having written them, not just the ones quoted but the entire number of them as they appear in the whole book which became a classic as soon as it was printed and immediately translated into several foreign languages. And although the author of this gem of English prose was not a Catholic, he often speaks with such sympathy for all that the Church teaches, that he can be safely numbered among those outside Her who was a Catholic in spirit. When I entered the Church, I discovered that this beautiful prose poem which I had been reading for years, was on the Index, so I went to my spiritual director who said to me these words: "I give you permission to read it."

As stated, instead of writing the story of my life I find myself getting lost in the great poetic truths of the world, the poetry life is. With Sir Thomas Browne, I too can say, "Now for my life, it is a miracle of" eighty-five years, which "to relate, were not a history, but a piece of poetry." Along this line, has it not been said that "St. Augustine was the greatet poet of antiquity who ever wrote a single line of verse," indicating that as a member of the household of the only true Church, his whole life became a poem.

But all of this has to stop and I must go on with the intent set out at the beginning, to write the story of my spiritual and intellectual life, made up of events and incidents which have long since passed into oblivion, so they have to be resurrected and re-lived and re-experienced in order to be expressed by words intelligent enough for others to read, and this means one has to know how to write them down, and which same knowledge is no small thing to have. It is for this reason I'd rather think of my life as a poem and not something prosaic and matter-of-fact and practical. I never did care too much for what was matter-of-fact, prosaic and practical, so it is for this reason I love the Church so much, transfiguring as She does, with Her sacramental system, everything into the supernatural and the divine.

It is the divine in the Church and the supernatural as well as Her whole mystical qualities which fascinate me so much and for which same I am so grateful to God. Where is one to find a religion with the riches the Church of Rome contains? Where can one go and find God present in His Sacramental state? What religion has produced such a vast variety of masterpieces of mystical theology? Where can we go to any of these religions and find a St. John of the Cross and a St. Teresa? It is for this reason I love the Church so much. I do so on account of the riches of Her interior life, Her great mystical treatises, Her inexhaustible wealth of supernatural doctrines and truths in relation to another form of existence, the one into which we shall enter immediately upon our departure from the one in which we now find ourselves. I love the Church because She never stops speaking of heaven to me, and of the Holy Eternity our Lord Himself is, for "He, Christ, is eternity," St. Bernard says to us. I love the Church because She speaks to me of the angels and saints in paradise and assuring me that I too will one day be with these angels and saints, so that what our Lord promised the good thief, She too is authorized to say to those by whom She is loved. I love the Church because She says to me

> I am the resurrection and the life:
> whoever believes in me,
> though he should die, will come to life;
> whoever is alive and believes in me will never die.
> (John 2:26)

I now come to a phase in my life already touched upon in the beginning of this narrative, and it has to do with the profound interest I have always had as regards the subject of mysticism and the experiences along that line had by nearly every saint whom the Church has canonized. To begin with, I had for many years before my conversion made a motto for myself in these words: "You can't refute a mystic," and I turned to, or rather was led by God to the field of mystical theology because it was by means of their mystical experience that all the men and women in the Church of Rome had risen to their highest heights in their experiences and relationship with their Savior and Redeemer. And also because it is in the mystical experiences had by all the saints the religious truths find their greatest ally and protector and safeguard and all of this because one cannot enter into a dialogue with someone who claims he or she had a personal experience of Christ and divine realities. You may not believe the mystic, but refute him by means of logical discussions, one cannot do. As I said, you either believe a mystic or you don't believe in him; argue with him along philosophical lines one cannot do, seeing that what the mystic experiences during mystical states cannot be described in any known way. The knowledge the mystic has of God is in the phrase of all the great mystical saints, a "knowledge knowledge." It is the "ray of darkness," quoted by St. John of the Cross, and so the human intellect cannot perceive what the soul experiences and much less attempt to describe what goes on in the soul's depth and substance. It is, as St. John of the Cross never tires of pointing out, "a touch of substances, of the substance of God in the substance of the soul" (*Living Flame of Love*, Stanza 2:21). As I said, and cannot repeat often enough, it is not my aim to write a treatise on mystical theology. But mystical experiences have played such a prominent part in my spiritual and intellectual life that something has to be stated in that regard, and I shall begin with the great *Commentary on the Book of Job* by St. Gregory the Great. When I first came across this monumental work, I was astounded at the wealth of thought it contained, so I began reading and re-reading it I don't know how often and how frequently. As I read this work, consisting of some two thousand pages, the realization came over me that the thoughts in it are so sublime that it would be useless to read it just once or twice, and that it had to be read continually and this for the period of many years. Fortunately there is a set of these books in the New York Public Library in its main branch, so I spent many years in that branch reading this wonderful sublime work of one of the greatest mystics who ever lived, and how happy I was to learn later on that this work was the favorite reading of both St. Thomas Aquinas and St. Teresa of Avila. I had read and re-read other works of mystical prayer such as the commentary on the Canticle of Canticles by St. Bernard, the Autobiography of St. Teresa, the works of St. John of the Cross; but it was the commentary of St. Gregory the Great which left a lasting influence on my prayer life. I have always felt that no one can read this great masterpiece of mystical spirituality and go on living the same spiritual life he had been practicing prior to his having read and re-read this sublime commentary.

Now, I said, I am not going to write a treatise on mystical theology, and I have every intention of adhering to this promise.

But mystical prayer has played such a vital role in my life as a Catholic, that something has to be stated that will point this out. I became interested in the writing of the great mystics the Church produced because of the realization that came over me that it is in the experiences of the great mystics the Church of Rome has alone produced that the greatest defence of the truths of Catholicism may be found. It is the mystics, as a great mystical theologian, Farges, says, that the early Church found its greatest protagonists. It is in the mystics that the faith of the early Christians shone most brightly, and it is in the same mystical writers that the faith of the Church has shone so brilliantly all throughout the Christian centuries. And so, as soon as I became Catholic, I immediately turned to the writings of the great mystical saints for strength and inspiration, so much so, that I feel I can't write the story of my prayer life, that is what this autobiography is all about anyway, without mentioning the debt of gratitude I owe to the writings of the great mystical saints I just mentioned, chief among these being St. Teresa of Avila and St. John of the Cross, and especially to the latter do I owe more than can be stated this side of heaven, because it is the writings of St. John of the Cross that really freed my soul so that it was no longer afraid to be led to the heights of prayer the contemplative life entails and carries with it.

It was the writings of St. John of the Cross that provided me with the assurance my soul had to have that it was on the right track in its efforts to attain union with God. It was due to his teachings I was not afraid to "launch out into the deep" of infused contemplative prayer, seeing the Church declared him to be an unerring guide along that line. In the Jesuit magazine *Stimmen der Zeit*, I read these German words as regards the importance of the writings of the Doctor of Mystical Theology St. John of the Cross has been declared by the Church to be:

Mit der Erhebung des hl. Johannes vom Kreuz zum Kirchenlehrer ist ein Wendepunkt für die mystische Theologie eingetreten. Denn in ihm haben wir fortan den sicheren, von der Kirche bestätigten Führer in mystischen Fragen zu sehen. Heute darf man sagen, dass die Auffassung des Heiligen vom Wesen der Mystik und das Beschauen die kirchliche ist.

(A. Mager, "Stimmen der Zeit")

I have in my poor broken German made an effort to translate these words so here they are for what they are worth:

> With the elevation of St. John of the Cross to Doctor of the Church, a turning point took place in the field of mystical theology. Today, we have to see in him the Church's sure guide in questions of mysticism. The saint's views of the nature of contemplation and mystical theology, are those of the Church.

The other day, someone put this question to me: "Why is God so far away?" To which question I replied with the words of St. Paul to the Corinthians: "Do you not realize that Jesus Christ is in you?" (2 Cor. 13:5 Revised Standard Version). Along this line how consoling it is to read the words of the Doctor of Mystical Theology when he speaks to us on this very same subject. "It brings," he says, "special happiness to a person to understand that God is never absent not even from a soul in mortal sin (and how much less from one in the state of grace)."

> What more do you want, O soul! and what else do you search for outside, when within yourself you possess your riches, delights, satisfactions, fullness, and kingdom—your Beloved whom you desire and seek. Be joyful and gladdened in your interior recollection with Him, for you have Him so close to you. Desire Him there, adore Him there. Do not go in pursuit of Him outside yourself. You will only become distracted and wearied thereby, and you shall not find Him, or enjoy Him more securely, or sooner, or more intimately than by seeking Him within you ·
> (*The Spiritual Canticle*, by St. John of the Cross,   Stanza I:8)

God is not far away from those who have the grace to be the blessed members of the only true Church, because for them, He is not only present from without, by means of the Sacrament of the Holy Eucharist. He is to be had in the substance of the soul when He is received in Holy Communion.

Let those outside the Church of Rome think of this when they find themselves unsatisfied with the partial truths contained outside the Church of Rome. For a Catholic, God in the Person of His Son, is close by. He cannot be more close by for such a person under the conditions of the present life, and to have our Lord closer to us than He is made possible to be when we receive Holy Communion, we have to depart from this life and enter into the state of glory, seeing it is only in the state of glory we can have our Lord and Savior in a more intimate way than we do by means of His sacramental presence in the Holy Eucharist.

There are today those among us who wrongly maintain that those outside the Church are also saved and which is most certainly true as Vatican II asserts a person can save his soul if that person does all he is able to find the truth and to seek for that truth with everything at his command. But look at all the graces such a person is deprived of by being outside the Church of Rome. Has such a person the consolation and strength that comes to us from visiting a Catholic Church where we can find Christ present in His Sacramental state? It was this realization of all she missed by remaining outside the Church of Rome which was responsible for the first American born woman to be raised to the altars of the Church and declared a saint.

The longer one stays in this life, the more one realizes that he cannot be fully satisfied until out of His great mercy and love God gives that person the grace to accept all that the Catholic Church teaches seeing that the fullness of God's revelation can be had in her alone.

Now, to get back to the question asked as to why God is so far away, the answer has already been given in the words of St. Paul, and in the Gospel of St. John we are told by our Lord Himself that having Him, we have His Father in heaven. No, God is not far away from those who do all they are given the grace to do, to seek and to find God where alone He may be had in all His fullness.

There was a time in the history of the world when God was far away. So out of the goodness of His Divine Heart He determined to get close to those whom He has fashioned in his own image and likeness and He did come closer, as close as our limited nature is able to endure the divine power of Almighty God. God became as the rest of us sin alone excepted. But what happened? There is no need to enter into the details of the Incarnation of Christ, because it is all of it retold in the four Gospels. God humbled Himself St. Augustine says, and man is proud. The people God loved most, and for whom He had done more than for any other nation, rejected Him, and we today are suffering the consequence of that rejection. For, had the entire Jewish race accepted Christ, who knows what benefit would have accrued to mankind as the result of their acceptance of Christ the Lord?

But as it is, only a handful of those He loved chose to rally round the Creator and Redeemer of the universe, and to them God is not far away but close by. So close by is God that if He were closer we could not go on living, the joy and the delight we would experience of His closeness to us would force the soul to take leave of its bodily habitation. In fact, it is possible that all that death is, is the sight of God in the state of glory, such a vision forcing the soul to leave the body and when this happens we say that so and so died. So and so merely was given a glimpse of all that God is in His majesty and beauty, and seeing the extent of this Majesty that the soul can no longer remain detained in a mortal body, it leaves the body and becomes assimilated to Christ, a mystical bond causing the two to become one.

We have God as close as we are able to have Him in the present life, and to have Him closer than we at present have Him, we have to die. The psalmist was given a vision of the beauty of the God Man, and he was so overcome and entranced by what he beheld, that he felt he could no longer remain in his mortal state. It was for this reason he said to our Lord,

> Lead me forth from prison,
> that I may give thanks to your name.
> (Ps. 142)

As the result of this vision, the psalmist felt he could not properly praise God in the present life, so he asked to be taken where this could be done, in the state of Glory.

Some of the most remarkable words ever written on the subject of death, are those of St. John of the Cross, as they are to be had in Stanza 11 of the Canticle of Canticles, for we there read:

> The soul does nothing very outstanding by wanting to die at the sight of the beauty of God in order to enjoy Him forever. Were she to have but a foreglimpse of the height and beauty of God, she would not only desire death in order to see Him now forever, as she here

desires, but she would very gladly undergo a thousand singularly bitter deaths to see Him only for a moment; and having seen Him, she would ask to suffer just as many more that she might see Him for another moment.

After reading these remarkable sublime words on the subject of death, one would despair having himself to write his own views on this great mystery, the mystery death will always be for a human being.

I know I am digressing from what I set out to write about. But, when we read the writings of the saints, we find them so beautiful, that we cannot resist the desire to wander about among these thoughts and this in the same way as when we walk in a garden of beautiful flowers, we don't know which ones we should gather up, seeing they are all of them endowed with their own special beauty. And so, when we start out writing down our own thoughts, we become distracted from doing so by the beautiful things we read in the writings of the saints. After reading what the mystical Doctor has to say on the subject of death, who is there who would not despair at any attempt to write down his own thoughts along this line?

Yes, I have certainly wandered far away from what I set out to put down in words, and answer the question asked of me as to why God is so far away. God was far away from me before I got the grace to detect Him being present not only close by, but to actually be in that part of myself made in His image and likeness, it was to that part of ourselves St. Paul was referring when he said, "Do you not realize that Jesus Christ is in you?" Yes, He is in that part of ourselves made in His Image—He is there in that part when we receive Him in Holy Communion, and this is a satisfaction and a consolation and a mystical experience, those outside the Church who reject her sacramental system cannot have, and so God is far away from them, and this due to no fault of His, but to the fact that multitudes prefer to remain outside the household of the only true faith as that only true faith is to be had in the Church of Rome. "Come unto me," in the Person of His Church, Christ says to all such, "Come to me, all you who are weary and find life burdensome, and I will refresh you" (Mt. 11:28). In part, these words may be interpreted to refer to the weariness of soul they experience who fail to seek for the truth where alone that truth may be had, and that fully, and not partially so, as in all the other religions of the world, in which the truths God wants us to have, can be found only to a limited degree and not completely. It is only the fullness of the faith as it is promulgated by the holy Roman Catholic Church that will appease the heart and mind of a human being. It is only the fullness of the truth that will satisfy him in his quest for the absolute.

I once walked into a Catholic Church and heard these words spoken by a priest from the pulpit: "Everyone in this Church tonight is going to go to purgatory." I did not at all see how this can compare with the psalmist saying that the "Mercy of God is above all his works," so I went to see my director and this is what he said to me: "A person can have the moral certainty of going to heaven without going to purgatory," and his words squared beautifully with those of the great St. Teresa: "All my longing then is to die; nor do I think about purgatory or of the great sins I've committed. . . . I am oblivious of everything in that anxious longing to see God" (*Life*, Ch. 10:13). I often think of these words and how consoling they are, not, of course, that I do not believe of going there and of the necessity there is to undergo purification to see God. But, as St. John of the Cross says, that "God does some people the favor of giving them their purgatory on earth," and so there is nothing amiss in believing one can go to heaven without going to purgatory, seeing all such have undergone their necessary purgation right here on this earth.

But, why am I saying all this in connection with the story of my life? I do so because I feel myself nearing the end of it, and so something should be stated about the glories of heaven into which the soul will one day be brought, and which in my case, cannot be too long, seeing I have reached the age of eighty-five. And as I said, how long can a person live anyway and how long should one even wish to live seeing that as soon as he will leave this world he will be immediately with God?

There is a passage in the biography of St. Teresa which should give us a great deal of consolation, it most certainly does me. It is quite lengthy, but it is of such a celestial nature that it should be quoted in its entirety. In it, she speaks of the graces her mystical experiences have produced in her:

> The revelations helped my very much, I think, in coming to know our true country and realizing that we are pilgrims here below; it is a wonderful thing to see what is there and know where we shall live. For if someone has to go to live permanently in another country, it is a great help to him in undergoing the struggle of the journey to have seen that it is a land where he will be very much at ease. These revelations are also a great help for reflecting on heavenly things and striving that our conversation be there; these things are done with ease. Doing them is very beneficial. Merely to look towards heaven recollects the soul, for since the Lord desired to reveal something of what is there, the soul concentrates on it. It happens to me some-times that those who I know live there are my companions and those in whom I find comfort; it seems to me that they are the ones who are truly alive and that those who live here on earth are so dead that not even the whole world, I think, affords me company, especially when I experience these impulses.
>
> (*Life*, Ch. 28:6)

Can we even imagine how enriched spiritually the lives of those in the Church would be if more Catholics would take these words to heart and have them before their mind's eye every now and then during their earthly existence. And is it not for this very reason that St. Francis de Sales said to the nuns he was directing these words: "We do not think enough of eternity," and by eternity he could have meant the joys that are laid up for us in the life to come, and of which same joys, if we thought suffi-cently of them, would they not serve to sweeten the bitterness of our earthly days? It was for this reason that as soon as I became a Catholic, I immediately turned to the writings of the great mys-tical saints like St. Teresa, St. John of the Cross, St. Gregory the Great, St. Bernard, St. Catherine of Siena, St. Gertrude the Great and so many men and women along this line, who were the blessed recipients of the favors from heaven, so as to in that way cheer and console those about them who have to put up with the trials of their earthly lot.

We need great and sublime souls in the Church, so it is for this reason we find one of them saying "Ordinary Catholics are plentiful enough; we need saints" (Fredrick Ozanam). In saying these words, Ozanam is merely repeating those of the psalmist when he lamented the fact that "there are no longer any saints on this earth." It is to be a saint that matters, not anything else one can achieve on this earth, and this no matter how important this may be. I have already stated that years ago, before I was a Catholic, I used to envy those who had made a great name for themselves in the world. When I became a Catholic, this envy ceased, for I got the grace to realize that great as anyone can become in achieving worldly successes, such success is nothing at all compared with the success of becoming a saint. And, everyone may if he so wishes become this kind of a success, since all such a one has to do is to ask God to give him or her the grace necessary by which this kind of success can be achieved. And, while I know only too well that all I have just said about becoming a saint may sound like preaching, I am not in the least apologetic along this line, and this because if there is any happiness to be had on this earth, the saints alone have this happiness and not ordinary Catholics. It is the saints who have kept the Church in existence; they have done so by the holiness of their lives, and it is to the saints like Teresa, we must go to get a living experience of what the joys of heaven are like—the saints experienced these joys so they alone can give us a taste of what they are like.

All of this is quite a digression from the aim which I set out to accomplish, to tell the story of my intellectual and spiritual life. But, as a Catholic, how can one speak of one's intellectual and spiritual life without going into detail to enumerate the qualities one's intellectual and spiritual life has to have in order for that life to be intellectual and to be genuinely spiritual in the supernatural sense of the words? So, it is for this reason that of being able to live an intellectual and spiritual life, that we have to have recourse to the writings of the saints, especially with those among them who were the blessed recipients of mystical graces, graces, that is, of infused supernatural prayer. And it is to mention all this I had to digress from the aim set for myself, seeing in speaking of the saints, we speak of Him who is the Saint of Saints, and speaking of Him, we do the only thing that's worthwhile doing.

In the fourteenth chapter of the *Life* of St. Teresa of Avila we find these revealing words:

The little time at my disposal is little help to me and so His Majesty must come to my aid. I have to follow the community life and have many other duties. . . . As a result, I write without the time and calm for it, and bit by bit. I should like to have time because when the Lord gives the Spirit, things are put down with ease in a much better way. Putting them down is like copying a model you have before your eyes. But if the spirit is lacking, it is more difficult to speak about these things than to speak Arabic, as the saying goes, even though many years may have been spent in prayer. As a result, it seems to me most advantageous to have this experience while I am writing, because I see clearly that it is not I who say what I write; for neither do I plan it with the intellect nor do I know how I managed to say it. This often happens to me.

I take the liberty to quote this long account of the way one of the world's greatest biographies was written. It was written with the aid of the Holy Spirit, and because it was thus written, the influence on the souls of those wishing to lead a deep prayer life is incalculable. As I read these words of St. Teresa, I wonder if it would be presumptuous of me to ask God's assistance in writing my own biography, because it is only when we have the assistance of God that we can accomplish something worthwhile in this life, so that the words of our Lord, "Without me you can do nothing," may also be applied to our literary efforts. It was in this way that the *Confessions* of St. Augustine have been written and perhaps the *Apologia Pro Vita Sua* of Cardinal Newman, for in these three biographies we have both literary genius as well as deep sanctity of life. I once said to someone that literary genius is not enough to procure for the mind and heart what God intends should be in that mind and heart, and that for that sanctity of life is also required. And so, when we read the biographies of the great saints who were both literary geniuses like these three and great saints, we find the power to move mountains of impediments to close union with our divine Lord. And, as I said, I wonder if it would be presumptuous of someone like myself to ask God to write the kind of story of my intellectual and spiritual life which would exert an influence for good on the lives of those who may read what I would like to say, what I would like to say is that unless we become saints, we miss everything that's worthwhile in the life of a human being. Along this line, let me cite the instance in which a friend of mine whom I knew for many years prior to my conversion, and who as a confirmed agnostic—the polite term for an atheist—in which this person said these words to me: "I believe that if there is any happiness to be had in this world, the only ones who have that happiness are the saints." It is good to call these words to mind, because they could have been spoken by a learned spiritual writer. And so, as I read the biography of St. Teresa of Avila, as I re-read it over and over for the course of many years, I ask myself this question: Why not let God help me express what's in the depth of my soul, since he can do this in a much more efficacious way, in a way that would be of help to souls.

I know full well that for such a task great sanctity of life is required, and it is only because St. Teresa was a saint that she was able to write with the unction that she did. But, unless we pray while we write why write at all, since the Holy Spirit will not be present in that writing, "If thou writest, thy composition has no charms for me, unless I read there the name of Jesus" (St. Bernard on the Canticle of Canticles, Sermon XV). What a wonderful thing it would be if those who write on the subject of prayer and the spiritual life would take these words of St. Bernard to heart!

But, I am digressing. I intended to write the story of my spiritual and intellectual life and here I am entering into the nature and essence of the great literary masterpieces which are spiritual classics. Still, it is good to digress if we have a gainful reason for doing so, and what could be more profitable to the soul than to bring up instances in the lives of the saints in which they gave to the world the great masterpieces of thought and prayer? What could be of more profit to the soul than to concern ourselves with the writings of the saints? Did not one of them (St. Philip Neri) actually say we should only read books by authors whose name begins with an "S." I concur wholeheartedly with this, for for the fifty-two years I have been in the Church the books I have read have, with rare exceptions, been the writings of the Fathers and Doctors of the Church, as well as those of the other saints whom the Church has raised to her altars.

And so, as I find myself re-reading the biography of St. Teresa of Avila, and this I don't know how many times I have already read and re-read this sublime work, I ask myself if it would not be presumptuous on my part to ask God that I too may merit His assistance in my effort to put down something of my prayer life which would be of help to those who may read what I would like to say along those lines. I would like to say that one of God's greatest gifts to me was the grace to be able to spend long hours of the day before His Eucharistic Presence on the altar, and that it was these prayers that helped me overcome the trials of my earthly lot, and to give me the grace to look forward to going home to heaven where I could be completely with Christ, even as St. Paul longed to be completely with Him when he said,

> Therefore, we continue to be confident. We know that while we dwell in the body we are away from the Lord. We walk by faith not by sight. I repeat, we are full of confidence and would much rather be away from the body and at home with the Lord.
> (2 Cor. 5:6-9)

These words are so sublimely beautiful that it is a wonder why we do not hear them spoken enough from our pulpits, seeing the consolation they bring with them would rejoice the hearts and minds of those who complain with the psalmist and say with him, "Woe is me that I sojourn in Meshech, that I dwell amid the tents of Kedar" (Ps. 120:5). The name Meshech denotes in Hebrew the idea of being long-drawn out and is in that language the root of a noun meaning Moses, who was thus named because he was drawn out of the water, Moses actually meaning to be "drawn out." And so, the soul here complains because our life in this world is so long-drawn out, for we would wish to be "freed from this life and to be with Christ, for that is the far better thing" (Philip. 1:23).

It is hard to go on in writing the story of one's spiritual and intellectual life, seeing there are so many aspects to that life, that one does not know on which one of these to dwell and which would be of greater interest to the reader, and of more help to him in his own prayer life. Still, one has to make an effort to go on, and ask God for the grace to do so, seeing we depend on His grace to know what to say and what not to say, which would be of relevance to the narrative as a whole. For God is always there to assist us in every need that can come up in a person's life, and all that is required is for that person to call upon God for His help, and this we certainly must do, seeing we are told to ask in order that we may receive, it is for God's grace we are to especially ask, and not so much the many temporal needs, for these will be given us if we first seek the kingdom of God Himself and the joys laid up for us in that kingdom as soon as we close our eyes in death, seeing as soon as we close our eyes in death we shall immediately be ushered into the Beatific Vision and with that Vision all our problems will be forever solved.

I just read, or re-read these words of St. Teresa: "O great secrets of God! I would never tire of trying to explain them if I thought I could in some way manage to do so; thus I will say a thousand foolish things in order that I might at times succeed and that we might give great praise to the Lord" (*Interior Castle*, VI). I sometimes feel the same way St. Teresa felt when I think of all I would like to say in reference to what I have started out doing by way of this autobiography. I too would say "a thousand foolish things" if I could in some way put down at least a small portion of the incidents and events which led to the conversion of my soul to the truths of our holy Catholic faith. Besides, does not St. Paul himself admonish us that we should be prepared to give a reason for the faith that's in us if we are asked to do so, and for a convert from Judaism this is always a frequent task, because when he speaks to a Catholic about his new-found faith, the very first question put to him or her is "what made you become a Catholic?" And yet, little does one realize what a stupendous thing it is to try even in the least way to give an adequate account as to how and in what manner a person goes about in getting himself disposed for the grace of God to bring about such a fundamental change in one's outlook on this as becoming a member of the household of the only true faith demands of that person.

In this connection I remember an incident in my life when I found myself in the presence of a Jewish rabbi who was very anxious to have me give him a reason as to why I became a Catholic. I realized the utterly monumental task such an effort would be, so I simply said thee words to him: "It was the result of an intimate experience of God." I knew this rabbi would not be satisfied with such a general answer to his question, but fortunately for me, he had to leave, so the conversation ended then and there. I say "fortunately" because it is always a deeply humiliating thing to try to tell someone of all that went on in one's heart and mind up to the time when, by the grace of God, such a person finds himself safely ensconsed in the treasury house of the truth the Church of Rome will always be for an enlightened human being. And it is for this reason that the words of St. Teresa of Avila now make such a deep impact on me, for, like her, I too would love to speak of the "secrets of God." I too, "would never tire of trying to explain them," the secrets of God in transforming someone's faith in Judaism to that of Catholicism, for that too constitutes one of the "secrets of God," one of the secrets of God's love for the soul in giving that soul the grace to be able to believe in all the truths the Church teaches, seeing the delight such belief brings with it and for which same truths a person is willing, and should be willing to lay down not only one single life but as many of them as God could give that person.

Yes, the conversion of one's soul to the Church of Rome will always constitute one of God's secrets, a secret of love for that soul in giving it the grace to be able not only to believe in, but love the truths of faith as they are promulgated by the Church of Rome.

And so, as one looks back at his spiritual and intellectual life, one gets the grace to marvel and be astonished at the goodness of God in His giving that person the gift of belief in the only true Church, a gift, which if that person had not had the grace to receive, it would have been in vain for that person to have been born, since without that person's ability to believe in the truths of faith, life for him would be as no life at all.

I know these are astounding words, but they more than merit them as far as I personally am concerned. As far as I personally am concerned, were I not a member of the household of the true faith the Catholic Church is, I would not want to go on living, since without such faith nothing on this earth would have any significance for me, and all its values would be no values at all, seeing it is the Church of Rome that endowed things with the value they have.

I don't know if I can go on much further along this line, so I will wait until I read some more of the sublime writings of St. Teresa of Avila and wait for these writings to inspire me what to say along deeply spiritual lines.

Along deeply spiritual lines we have to go to the writings of the saints, since in them alone we will receive the full insight in things divine—the saints alone speak to us in deeply supernatural terms, so to have a living experience of all God is like, and of all that is waiting for us in the life to come, for such a purpose we have to go to the writings of the saints, they alone speak of things divine in the way and manner we can strengthen our own belief in what is of a transcendent nature, and which surpasses the power of the mind to comprehend. And so as I get the grace to read the writings of St. Teresa of Avila, I look forward to the time when I too will have something worthwhile to say along deeply spiritual lines, and this in connection with the grace of being enabled to believe in all that the Church teaches and for which reason God gave me the grace to become a member of Her Mystical Body, the Mystical Body of Christ the Church of Rome will always be, so that in order to be united to Christ one had to be united to Him whose Mystical Body she blessedly is. In the words already quoted from St. Gregory the Great, "The Church and Christ are one Person," that is to say, the Church is Christ and Christ is the Church, and that without her for his Mother, one cannot have God for his Father, at least this is what the Fathers of the Church have always unanimously maintained, so that what was good enough for them should be good enough for us as well, seeing that closer to the Heart and Mind of Christ than the Fathers had been one cannot come.

There is an important phase in my prayer life which I feel should be gone into with more detail than had hitherto been done. So I will do so by means of a letter I had written to someone whose spiritual and intellectual life has had a profound influence on me since the very first time God arranged the two of us should meet—Ronda Chervin. Ronda Chervin is scheduled to give a series of talks on the writings of St. John of the Cross, so I figured it would be of help to her to know the influence the writings of St. John of the Cross had on my own spiritual life and this for the fifty years I have been in the Church. So, without further explanation, I am including this letter to her in this biography:

Dear Ronda:

For a period of many years, I have always wanted to write something about St. John of the Cross by way of expressing my gratitude to him for his helping me to pray the way I have been doing since I entered the Church. But every time I tried to do this I could not succeed, and perhaps this was due that I had no strong motivation for that kind of task. But now that you are going to give a series of talks on him, maybe I should start trying to give you some idea of all he has meant to me all these years, so I will begin with an experience of him I had years before the thought of becoming a Catholic, and even a Christian, ever not only took root in my mind but it did not even occur to me. One day, I was browsing through shelves of a branch of the New York Public Library, and as I did so I picked up a book with this strange title, *The Dark Night of the Soul.* In those days, before I began reading a book on serious subjects, the first thing I did was to look and see if that book had an Imprimatur in it, for if it did, I knew that such a book would do me intellectual harm. Naturally, a work like this had such an Imprimatur, so without bothering to look through its contents, I placed it back on the shelf from which I took it. Still, the title of this book kind of haunted me—what can be meant by the "Dark Night of the Soul?" So I picked up the book and began looking through some of its contents, and as I did so, I began to get real scared. I was scared to find things in it which I felt I had myself experienced for many years. I was a bit frightened at the thought that a Church I disliked so much, and which I did not trust, should have someone in her who would write about the kind of experience I had myself undergone. With time, though, these fears, although they did not completely disappear, lessened considerably, so I began to read more of its contents until I covered the entire book. Years passed, and I forgot about this incident until I became a Catholic, and heard some people say that not everyone should read the writings of St. John of the Cross. So I immediately went to see Fr. Clark and asked what view I should hold as regards his writings, and the answer he gave was, "There is nothing more sublime outside the Scriptures."

There is nothing more sublime outside the Scriptures, and there most certainly is not. When I found myself spending long hours in church, I felt a little uneasy. I was kind of afraid of letting myself be absorbed in God. I was afraid that during these long periods of prayer, something might happen to me mentally. So when I began to read all St. John of the Cross has to say along lines of prayer, infused prayer, and mystical graces of every variety, the fear I had was turned into confidence. I began to have confidence in my prayer life, and all of this due to having read and re-read everything St. John of the Cross has written. I have re-read all of his writings so often during the fifty years I have been in the Church, that I have the substance of all he has to say along lines of infused contemplative prayer in the substance of the soul, so much so, that I don't even feel that I have to read him anymore.

Still, for the sake of precaution, not a year goes by I do not re-read his complete works, and I know of no writer on prayer whose teachings I have followed more closely than those of St. John of the Cross, for he it was, who more than any other writer on that subject I have read, assured and reassured me that I was on the right path as far a this kind of prayer is concerned. St. John of the Cross gives me this assurance, because there is no single detail in the contemplative state he does not deal with in precise terms. In fact, someone said that where all the other mystics in the Church leave off, he begins, and the more thoroughly I read his writings the more thoroughly I agree with this statement. And is it not due to his deep insight into the nature of mystical prayer that he has been declared Doctor of Mystical Theology?

I have often felt that were it not for the fact of having soaked myself in the writings of St. John of the Cross I could not have lived the prayer life I felt it is God's will for me to live, and this feeling has been confirmed for me by the two greatest spiritual directors this Province of the Society of Jesus has produced, Fr. William Clark, S.J. and Fr. Joseph McFarlane, S.J. I once had lunch with one of the most outstanding spiritual directors there was, Fr. Keenan, S.J., and when Fr. Clark's name came up, this great director said these words to me: "He," meaning Fr. Clark, "was the dean of them all." These words coming from someone who was himself such an outstanding spiritual director, had a deep impact on me and made me admire Fr. Clark even more than I had done so.

I mention all this to you because it was Fr. Clark who confirmed my desire to give myself completely to God by way of contemplative prayer, the kind of contemplative prayer St. John of the Cross, more than anyone else in the Church, writes about with such precision, and profundity. No one has ever spoken about God in such a sublime way, no one has ever made Him so real and so vivid to the soul. So when you are going to give talks on the writings of St. John of the Cross, know you'll never meet anyone in this life for whose prayer life these writings have done more than they for me during all the fifty years I have been in the Church, and had I not soaked myself in these writings I don't know what my prayer life would today be, how this prayer life of mine could be without his writings, I cannot even imagine and try to figure out, seeing it was St. John of the Cross whom I took for an unerring guide along the steep paths of mystical prayer and mystical contemplative life. Tell this to the Sisters you are going to give the talks to. Let them know you know of no one who owes more to St. John of the Cross than I am graced by God to owe him. Without him, I would not be the kind of person it is God's will for me to be in a spiritual way.

Love,
Charlie

The biography will be finished when I get to heaven—its purpose is to lead to that sacred abode. In a letter to the person who was directly responsible for her conversion, we find these words: "You have led me to a happiness which admits of no description." Every convert is, by means of his conversion, led to this kind of happiness. So it is for this reason he can never sufficiently thank God for such an extraordinary favor and grace, a favor and grace which is only second to the gift of his existence. And as has already been stated, it would in my case have been in vain to have been born had God not been good enough to extend me the grace to become a member of the Mystical Body of Christ the Church of Rome is. Without the Life Christ is, there is no life at all, and for him also the Life Christ is can only be had where he now so blessedly is.

I said the biography will be finished when I get to heaven, because it is there only the summation of our earthly existence will take place. The psalmist tells us that:

> heaven is the heaven of the Lord,
> but the earth he has given to the
> children of men.
> (Ps. 115:16)

Before the sin of our first parents the earth was itself a kind of paradise. It is to restore us to our paradisal state that God became Man. It is for heaven we have been made and for no other earthly good thing. It is to heaven every good and beautiful experience points and has in view.

I became a Catholic so that I may in that way be happy, not just for a few years, but forever and ever. I became a Catholic that I may in that way get the grace to one day participate in the joys of the angels and saints in the life to come. It is to that life the grace of conversion is meant to lead. It is meant to lead to a happiness we cannot now imagine or conceive.

No, it is not for this life alone we are Catholics. We are Catholics that by being so we may get the grace to live the Life Christ Himself is and which same can never have a limit to it. It is for the Boundlessness they are in who have left the world we have been born. Does not St. Paul say that "if our hopes in Christ are limited to this life only, we are the most pitiable of men" (I Cor. 15:19). We have not been born to be happy on earth. "I do not promise to make you happy in this life but in the next," the Blessed Virgin said to St. Bernadette. "Do not promise yourself what Christ did not promise you," St. Augustine said to those of his own day. He repeats these words to us: "What Christ has promised," this Doctor of the Church tells us, "is not of this world." I did not become a Catholic to be happy in the present life but in the one to come, my holy Catholic faith being a ticket to the eternal and everlasting kind of joys they experience who are now in heaven. It is the heaven of unimagined bliss my becoming a Catholic had in view. It is not of earth my holy Catholic faith speaks to me. It does so of the transcendent Good Jesus can alone be for a human being.

And so, one can write and write and write about the story of one's conversion and never come to an end. He can never come to an end of enumerating the blessings conferred upon him by the grace of his becoming a Catholic. "The favors of the Lord I will sing forever" (Hebrew: "mercy"; Ps. 89:2). What mercy of the Lord can exceed the mercy of God enabling me to be able to believe in all the Catholic Church teaches? Can the mercy of God be made more manifest in the grace extended to us to become a member of the only true Church? It is becoming a Catholic that matters and not in any other thing the world has to offer be this good and beautiful as it may. The Church of Rome gives us God Himself. It does so in all His fullness—a greater gift than God is, a human being cannot hope to receive. We receive the gift God

Himself is when we receive Holy Communion. Can Protestant-ism and Judaism endow the soul with such a sublime gift? It is to the Church we must go to have God in the fullness He may be experienced by us this side of heaven. To become more inti-mately united with God the Church enables us to be by means of her Holy Sacraments, we must take leave of this life. It is Christ the Church gives us as he may be had under the conditions of the present life. To have God in all His fullness we have to have the grace of membership in His Mystical Body. It is the Voice of Christ the Church makes use of when He says "I came that they might have life and have it to the full" (Jn. 10:10).

The day I was inducted into the army during World War II, part of the ritual was to undergo examination by two pyschia-trists, so one of them asked me this question: "Do you get depressed?" to which I answered no. The next question was, "Were you depressed in the past?" I said yes. "Why aren't you depressed now?" "Because I am a Catholic," was the answer I gave, and this brings me to the whole question of happiness and unhappiness and as to the reason for them both. As I said, I was very unhappy prior to receiving the gift of faith in the only true Church, and this so much so that I not only thought of putting an end to my existence but actually took measures to bring it about. All of this indicating the profound change conversion to the Catholic faith brought about in my life, so it is for this reason alone I cannot thank God enough and pray He give the same gift of faith to all those I know and love, especially to the members of my family, not to my mother, because being in heaven she no longer has any need for the faith by which we who are not yet where she blessedly is, have to have to sustain our existence on this earth.

As I keep writing this autobiography, I often reach a stage where I don't know how to go on. So when that comes about, I make a sign of the Cross and continue on typing. I often feel someone in heaven is helping me do what I am along this line, and this is as it should be, seeing I know so many who are already in the state of blessedness in which we who are not yet there hope one day to be. A biography such as this, has to be written with the help of prayer, since without such assistance, what one has to say will have no lasting value. There are many books being written today which, in a few years from now, will no longer be available, so it is not such a book it is my intention to write. Along this line, there is a beautiful expression in Goethe's *Faust* which is almost impossible to translate so it has to be quoted in the original:

Was glänzt, ist für den Augenblick geboren,
Das Echte bleibt der Nachwelt unverloren.

Bayard Taylor has rendered these words as follows:

What dazzles, for the moment spends its spirit:
What's genuine, shall posterity inherit.
(*Faust*, Prelude)

In my own way, I have always tried to interpret the meaning of these words to signify that it is only that which has depth and genuineness that remains for future generations to ponder, and investigate, and reflect upon, because that which is superficial in its nature, has a short-lived existence, such as many of the books now published and read by the millions of superficially minded readers, and it is for no such I intend to write. In fact, why write about something which in a few years from now nobody will take the trouble to read, seeing everything in that writing is dated, so it has absolutely no relevance to the problems those will have who will live years from today, and this, these future generations Goethe has in view when he says that *Das Echte*, the genuine which has lasting value, *bleibt der Nachwelt*, future generations, *unverloren*, a word which signifies something that has about it the value of permanence which all great literary masterpieces have about them, so it is for this reason they are continued being read for centuries after they had been written. Can anyone imagine that the time will come when people will stop reading the poetry of Homer, Dante, Shakespeare and Goethe? One cannot: and so it is this what is meant by the beautiful words the greatest poet Germany produced has written.

I have digressed but this digression has served a good purpose, so I am in no way sorry it was made. In writing about one's spiritual and intellectual life, one has to traverse territories that have no bounds set to their variety and extent. It is like writing about what has a beginning but which will never have an end. The life of a human being has a beginning, being that that human being has been made in the image of God, how can that human being have an end? Can the image of God in which that human being has been made, ever come not to be that which it is, something eternal and divine? And is it not due to the fact that a human being has been made in God's image that we're commanded by Him who made that human being, to be loved with the same love with which we love the Maker of him and our own selves? There is a beautiful line in the poetry of Edmund Spenser which I cannot avoid the temptation to quote: "Images of God in earthly clay."

Yes, it is an arduous task to write about one's spiritual and intellectual life, so that without the assistance of God's grace this cannot be done—it is God who has to give us the grace to know what we should write about, and this as the story of one's life grows in length and in depth.

A few minutes ago, I was speaking about the subject of happiness and unhappiness and how the former can only be had by a person whose intent is to carry out God's holy will, and that without that intent, it is in vain we look for happiness on this earth. In fact, St. Augustine says that there is no one who does not seek to be happy; but he seeks for happiness in the wrong place. The adulterer, this Doctor of the Church says, seeks for his happiness in his adultery, so it is for this reason he finds misery in the place of genuine felicity. We all of us seek our own good; but we do not seek for that good where alone it may be had—in the Church of Rome. Prior to my conversion I too was seeking for my happiness where, as the result of the bitter experience I went through, I learnt with pain and anguish the happiness I sought cannot be found. I sought for happiness in the things made by God and not in the Maker of them. And, while as St. Augustine never fails to remind us, it is not wrong to love the things God has made, and that what is wrong is to depend on what God has made for blessedness, seeing blessedness, something for which we have been brought into the being we have, can only be had in the Infinitely Blessed One Christ is and the Church He founded.

In the first psalm, we read these words: "Happy the man who follows not the counsel of the wicked, nor walks in the way of sinners," etc. Now, it is of interest to note that the word "happy" in the Hebrew denotes someone who is well-off in a material way and who is in possession of great wealth. In the Hebrew, the word "blessed" is akin to the root which could signify a person who is a millionaire, for virtue and riches denote the same things in the Hebrew. Thus indicating that it is the virtuous man who is really and truly well-off, and not the person who does not live a life in accordance with God's holy will. It is that man of virtue who is well-off in the eyes of God, and from the point of view of the next life, along this line, does Augustine say, "not yet have you the wealth of the angels." Not yet do we have the riches of Christ which consist in the grace to live a life in perfect accordance with God's holy will, seeing it is only when we get the grace to live lives of holiness that we are happy and well-off and in no other way, and this even if we could possess the whole world of material riches. And so when the psalmist tells us that "Happy the man who follows not the counsel of the wicked," he means to indicate that it is only those who live lives in accordance with God's will who can be called "happy". They, and no other types of human beings, rich as they may be in this world's goods to which St. Paul refers with the word, "rubbish" (Phil. 3:8). In the eyes of God, everything which is not of a nature to last forever is not worth giving a thought, much less something for which to labor and expand one's energy to acquire with so much pain and anguish.

"I do not understand why people want to live," St. Teresa said, "since everything is so uncertain." St. Teresa could not understand why people do not want to be where everything *is* certain, in the state of glory. I have always felt the same way, especially since my conversion. As soon as I was baptized, this is the thought that came to me: the gates of heaven have been opened for me by the grace of baptism, so why remain in a world like this? Why not enter through the portals of paradise which after having been shut by sin, have been opened up for me by the grace I received to become a Catholic? There are some who falsely teach that the Jewish people do not have to undergo conversion to the Catholic faith, and this is something I will never be able to understand. I will never be able to understand such false teaching for the simple reason that before my conversion I was one sort of person and I am now since my conversion a completely different kind of a person, the transformation having been brought about by the grace of baptism.

Yes, I was one kind of person before I became a Catholic and by the grace of God I am now a completely different kind of a person, and all of this because of my firm belief in the existence of another life than the one in which I now so sadly find myself, so far away from the happiness they experience who are now in heaven. Faith in Christianity having opened for me the gates of heaven, I find it a trial to go on living in a world filled with so much sin and evil, chief among this sin being lack of belief in all that the Church teaches as regards our home in heaven.

The grace of conversion has made me a different kind of a person from a spiritual and intellectual point of view, so I can never thank God enough for His goodness in enabling me to now be that person that I am, one who has the grace to love Christ to an excessive degree as well as to love the Church of Christ, seeing, He, Christ, and the Church constitute one Person.

Yes, I can never thank God enough for extending me the grace to become a Catholic, and the first thing I will do when I get to heaven will be to thank Him for the gift of becoming a member of the Mystical Body of Christ the Church of Rome will always be. Some people glory in being materially well-off, while there are others who rejoice in fame and honor. As far as I am concerned, I am unable to find satisfaction in anything other than in the realization of my being what I am, a member of the household of the one true faith. It is sad to see so many Catholics take their faith in the Church for granted and not thanking God for that faith and doing so every moment of their earthly days. It is sad to see so many Catholics not filled with rapturous delight at the realization of their being the blessed members of the Church of Rome. I read the story of a little boy standing near the entrance to a diamond mine. He had a stick in his hand with which he kept pushing in the mud what seemed to be a chunk of stone but which turned out to be a precious diamond. Some people do the same thing with their Catholic faith. They fail to realize the infinite worth of a faith for which millions of men and women and even children have already received the grace to lay down their lives. And this is a tragedy of the first order, the one lack of appreciation being a Catholic will always be. Can we glory in anything better than in the hope we have that after this life will be over we shall be inconceivably happy? To how many has been given the grace to be in rapturous awe at the realization that they are the blessed members of the only true Church? How many rejoice at the thought of being a Catholic? If they did, how happy they should be, seeing they would in a realization of heaven's joys "Taste and see how good [Hebrew, "sweet"] the Lord is" (Ps. 39:14). We get such a taste of the sweetness of Christ every time we call to mind the gift of faith in the supernatural and the divine. We get a taste of the sweetness of Christ when we call to mind all God has done for us by giving us the grace to believe all the Church teaches. Can there be anything sweeter a human being can experience in this life than the thought of being a Catholic, seeing that in this thought all of heaven's joys are contained? We think of heaven's joys when we call to mind the Church of Rome, seeing it is these joys she proclaims and promulgates.

The Church exists to assure us that after this life will be over we shall be inconceivably happy. The devil hates joy of heart so he does everything allowed him by God to remove that joy from our hearts. It is the devil's aim to make us miserable, and he does this by suggesting to people that there is no objective basis for the faith we love. It is—to destroy the Church of Rome—the mission the devil has set for himself. And hating the Church, he hates Christ the Founder thereof.

> Why do the nations rage
> and the people utter vain folly?
> The kings of the earth rise up,
> and the princes conspire together
> Against the Lord and against his anointed.
> (Ps. 1:1)

It is to Christ these words have reference. It is His kingdom of joy in the heart and mind of a human being. Christ came to undo the devil's work. He appeared on earth for no other purpose. It is unbelief in the truths of faith the devil has to offer to all those who have the misfortune to make themselves his willing slaves. Slavery has been abolished by the United States Government, but not the slavery sin will always bring with it.

In a little notebook of mine in which I put down the sayings of the saints, I just came across these words: "Anyone who refuses to believe in the divinity of our Lord Jesus Christ cannot help but demean himself. It were better not to have been born than not to believe in the divinity of our Lord Jesus Christ." I have since my conversion never failed to have these words in my inmost being. And yet, when you speak this way to some people who should know better, they look at you as if you just uttered a heretical remark of the first order. And yet, no matter how much men will ignore the fact that in the above words it "were better not to have been born than not to believe in the divinity of our Lord and Savior Jesus Christ," these words will always remain true and they will continue to haunt that part of the human race which has knowingly and willfully rejected belief in the divinity of Christ, seeing the sin of unbelief is one which can only be forgiven by the Holy Spirit.

When our divine Lord was suspended on the cross, one of the sources of the anguish He went through was His foreknowledge that there will always be those among whom He will always love, who will stubbornly and consistently refuse to believe in His divinity and among these are those of every race and creed. There are many things which we do that are contrary to God's holy will, such as the sins we commit with our bodily being. These may be excused on account of the frailty of human nature. But there is no one who has to refuse to believe in the divinity of Christ when God gives that person the grace to be able to accept the teaching of the Church along this line.

How it will always break the hearts of the saints to see people refuse to love the Love Itself Jesus is! Was it not this refusal that broke the Heart of Christ? "Woe is me, there are no more any saints on this earth," the psalmist says in one of his psalms. The saints of God keep on repeating these words and they will continue on repeating them until the very end of the end of all things.

Hear, O heavens, and listen, O earth,
for the Lord speaks:
sons have I raised and reared,
but they have disowned me!
An ox knows its owner,
and ass its master's manger;
But Israel does not know.
My people have not understood.
(Is. 1:2-3)

And while these words have been spoken by Christ two thousand years ago to the people He loved most, they are continued to be spoken in reference to those who, for the sake of worldly conveniences and worldly pleasures, desert the Church of Rome and especially those who have been endowed with the grace of a religious vocation. Christ's Heart continues to be broken and so it has to be assuaged by those who have been given the grace to love that Heart for those who do not wish to know the secrets of love that Heart contains. There are those among the nations of the world who will always refuse to believe in the divinity of Christ, and this will always constitute an outrage and scandal of the first order, seeing there is no bodily infirmity to excuse us from our not being able to carry out the commandment to love our Lord with our whole heart, with our whole mind and with all our strength. And so, when we are confronted with the sin of unbelief, we are forced to consider this to be the worst form of evil the world will always be guilty of having.

I know I have digressed from the aim I have set out to write the story of my spiritual and intellectual life. But, as I think of all the unbelief that is in the world today and of the mercy of God to have the grace not to offend Him in this respect, I simply have to express my view along this line. We just can't stand by and see all this unbelief being so prevalent in the world and not be grieved over it as were all the saints. Hasn't the great St. Teresa herself told us that she was not upset by any sins that men commit except the one heresy and unbelief are. And so like her, we too should only be upset by the sins of the mind and not so much committed by the frailty of our human nature, seeing these latter are in no way as grievous as are the former. I can understand any sin a human being can commit, because I have before my conversion been guilty of them myself. But what I will never be able to understand how a human being made in the image of God can fail to love the Love Itself Jesus is. This is something altogether too baffling and too perplexing and too mysterious for my limited intelligence to try to figure out. And was it not for this reason, the lack of love for Love Itself, that made St. Mary Magdalen go about the convent halls crying out and saying aloud that "Love is not loved?" And, is there, can there be, a more lamentable sight in this world than to see people fail to love the Love Itself Jesus is?

As I have said, I started out writing the story of my conversion, but I cannot pass by something I have experienced as a Catholic which has caused me deep pain—it consists in seeing people defect from the Love Jesus is. They defect from a Church which is suffused with the love for Christ, so they defect from the love Itself Christ is, and this for the reason of our Lord being able to be fully appreciated, fully known and fully loved in the Church of Rome, seeing that when we leave Rome we leave Him who constitutes the nature and essence of all Rome is meant to be, it is the Church of Rome our Lord has appropriated for His Bride. It is her he has drawn so close to His own blessed being that she has become mystically, one with all He Himself is.

This whole subject concerning those who fail to love the Love Itself Jesus is, is getting too baffling to try to figure out, so we will have to wait for heaven to find out why our Lord will always have so many Judases in the Church founded by Him. There will always be those who both knowingly and unknowingly break the Heart of Christ and breaking the Heart of Christ they break the heart of the Mother of Christ the Church of Rome will always be, though she will always be that in a mystical way. I once met a holy religious and when I did, I asked what she thought of all those who are leaving the Church and this is the answer she gave "They do not leave; the Holy Spirit removes them."

The longer we stay in this life and the closer we draw to God the more keenly we realize that we are in our exile on this earth and not in our native land the native land heaven is for the soul of a human being. And it is not of my home I write in this autobiography but of my exile in it. There is a beautiful passage in the *Life* of St. Teresa of Avila in which she speaks of the exile she felt herself to be in all the time she so sadly found herself away from the home of the soul Christ in the state of glory is. "If someone like myself," she says, "often feels so strongly the fact of my exile, I at times wonder what the feeling of the saints must have been. What must St. Paul and the Magadalen and others like them have undergone, in whom the fire of the love of God had grown so intense? It must have been a continual martyrdom." We can answer very easily what they must have felt and we do this in the words of St. Paul, seeing that in Chapter 5, Verse 6 of his Second Epistle to the Corinthians he has this to say: "Therefore we continue to be confident. We know that while we dwell in the body we are away fom the Lord . . . and would much rather be away from the body and be at home with the Lord." I know this passage has already been quoted in another part of this autobiography, but it is of such importance that we cannot sufficiently call it to mind, seeing every time we do so, a consolation from heaven enters into our inner being. Every time we call words of St. Paul to mind we are made to realize that we are exiles on this earth, and so we look forward to our one day departing from it so that we will be "at home with the Lord."

And it is not only the Christians who longed for their home in heaven but the Jews too, for we find them saying; "By the streams of Babylon we sat and wept, when we remembered Zion" (Ps. 137:1). Now, Zion stands for our home in heaven and not for anything that can be had in this present life. It is for their home in heaven the prophets of old longed and not for what can be had under the conditions of the present life. And we too, complain with the Jews of old; we too say with them, "By the streams of Babylon we sat and wept, when we remembered Zion," Zion also signifying the joys to come and it in no way has any kind of reference to the things that pass away with time.

Perhaps someone, as he reads this biography, may accuse me of taking refuge in quoting the words of others instead of trying to make use of my own expressions. But what more beautiful things can be said than those which have already been written by the inspired writers both of Holy Writ itself and by those who received the grace to penetrate into its secret depths, like St. Augustine and all the other Fathers and Doctors of the Church? We cannot improve on the writings of the saints, so let us not try to do so. Where can we find more beautiful words with which to express our own thoughts along deeply spiritual lines? We cannot, is the answer we must give, seeing it is in the writings of the saints we find the unction with which to speak of divine things and not among those who are devoid of holiness of life.

I sometimes feel an autobiography should be a kind of spiritual and intellectual mirror in which one can look and see a reflection of his own inner being. Also, others too should be able to look into that kind of a mirror and they too should be able to see the reflection of the inner being of the person they read about so that an autobiography may serve a double purpose. Also, one may sometimes wonder if it is vanity and vainglory that prompts people to write an autobiography of their spiritual and intellectual lives, and if it is vanity, then we have to accuse some of the greatest human beings like St. Augustine and others equally dear to the Heart of Christ, of the same motive, and this would be a preposterous thing to do. No, it is love for Christ that motivates people like him and St. Teresa of Avila and Cardinal Newman to disclose themselves to others by the story of their spiritual and intellectual lives. And so we should thank God for having given St. Augustine the grace to write one of the world's great masterpieces in the form of his *Confessions,* a book I carried about my person for ten years before I became a Catholic. And, there is the *Life* of St. Teresa of Avila and this too I had the grace to read for many years prior to my conversion. And then comes the *Apologia Pro Vita Sua* of Cardinal Newman, and it is in heaven I will be able to fully realize all I owe to these three spiritual and intellectual masterpieces. Where would I today be without the influence these three giants of the faith exerted over my mind and heart and this many, many years before I even thought I would one day get the grace to believe in all the truths that the Church is commissioned by God to teach and promulgate.

As I said, an autobiography should be a kind of spiritual and intellectual mirror in which the author of the biography should every now and then get a glimpse of his own inner being, so as to thank God for the riches He has instilled into that inner being. By writing an autobiography we get the grace to enable others to receive a glimpse at all that goes on in that part of our make-up made in the image of God. And we may be consoled and strengthened by what is there made manifest. Along this line, does not St. Paul say somewhere that no man lives for himself, so that the lives we live belong not only to our own selves. It is to Christ our lives belong and to the members of His Mystical Body.

I think of all this as I find myself giving an account of my spiritual and intellectual life. I think of the effect of what I write on those who read what I have to say. And, like St. Augustine, I too would rather read what others have written than to write myself. But there is the obligation of gratitude to make known to others how merciful God has been to me by giving me the grace to be able to believe in all that the Church teaches, so that with the psalmist "Thy favors [Hebrew: "grace, kindness, mercy"] I will sing forever" (Ps. 89:2), since it is due to the mercy of the Lord that I am a Catholic, and being one, I pray this kind of grace should be extended to all the others who find themselves outside the household of the only true faith. With St. Paul, "I speak the truth in Christ: I do not lie. My conscience bears me witness in the Holy Spirit that there is great grief and constant pain in my heart. Indeed, I could even wish to be separated from Christ for the sake of my brothers, my kinsmen the Israelites" (Rom. 9:1-5). With the apostle to the gentiles, I especially pray for my fellow Jewish brothers. I do so that they too should get the grace to enter into the fullness of God's revelation as it stands revealed both in the Old and the New Testaments. Does not Irenaeus say that "the words of Moses are the words of Christ"? Soon, I at least, will be not in the eternity of the philosophers and the metaphysicians but in God's holy eternity, in the eternity which St. Bernard says Christ is. "He, Christ, is Eternity," this Doctor of the Church goes on to state.

Even the pagans believed in the existence of another world. But for reasons known to God, it is only to the members of Christ's Mystical Body that He has revealed all that is waiting for us in the life to come. It is to this Church of Rome that a vision has been given of the joys awaiting us as soon as we close our eyes in death, seeing that as soon as we close our eyes in death, we shall be completely with Christ in the completeness of which St. Paul speaks when he says, "Therefore while we dwell in the body we are away from the Lord...and would much rather be away from the body and be at home with the Lord" (2 Cor. 5:6-8). It is only to the Church of Rome that a vision has been given of the heavenly Jerusalem. It is only to her members that that was disclosed which they experience who are now in heaven. It is not earth the Christian wants but the counterpart heaven is. For, "the earth," a saint said (Realino) "is not the Christian's home; let those who want it have the earth." Those who love Christ long for the heaven of infinite bliss Jesus is.

> My soul yearns and pines
> for the courts of the Lord;
> My heart and my flesh
> cry out for the living God.
> (Ps. 84:3)

St. Paul tells us that he wants to be "freed from this life and to be with Christ" (Phil. 1:23), and the psalmist tells us the same thing in different words:

> Lead me forth from prison,
> that I may give thanks to your name.
> (Ps. 142:8)

These words are written to instruct us that we cannot adequately praise God in the present life and that in order to do so, we have to die, so as to in that way enter into the "joys of the Lord." *Ich liebe dich O Ewigkeit* ("I love thee, O Eternity") Nietzsche said, but he is in these words not referring to the *Ewigkeit*, to the Eternity Jesus is. All the saints longed for heaven. They have all of them longed to be with Christ in the state of glory. With St. Gregory the Great, they held that the "Righteous man is weary to live." Now, if the "righteous man is weary to live," are not they unrighteous who desire to live a long time in a world like this, so as to in that way be far away from Christ in the state of glory? We don't know what the answer to this question is, seeing many of God's greatest saints lived a long time on this earth and performed deeds of virtue all the time they were on the earth.

The proper attitutde of those who love Christ is to stay in this life as long as it is God's holy will for us to do so. What matters is to want to be with Christ in the state of glory and not whether we live a long time or a short one all the days we are away from the Beatific Vision. And this because it is Christ that matters and no other thing God has made—has it not been said to us "This is my beloved Son. My favor rests on him" (Mt. 3:17) and "God so loved the world that he gave his only Son" (Jn. 3:16), indicating in all of this it is Christ we must long for every single moment of the twenty-four hour day and that it is this holy longing which endears us to His Father in heaven.

Yes, it is Christ the Lord we long for and as He may be experienced in the state of glory, since it is in that state that satisfaction will be given to all our God-instilled desires. "On waking, I shall be content in your presence" (Ps. 7:15). The Septuagint version has this interesting rendition of these words: "I shall be satisfied when thy glory appears," the Hebrew for "satisfied" implying the idea of satiety, having in excess, surfeited, to have one's fill, and so on.

And so as we think of all this, the conviction we arrive at is that we have been made for another and infinitely more beautiful life than the one in which we now find ourselves and only in that life the goal of our hearts' desires will be attained, the goal in the state of glory Jesus is. No, "earth is not the Christian's home," so "let those who want it have the earth" who have not received a taste on earth of what the joys of heaven are like. Those who have received such a taste want to be with Him from whose bounty this taste came to us. "Taste and see how good [Hebrew: "sweet"] the Lord is" (Ps. 34:9) and in which words our Lord is here speaking to us of His own Blessed Self and the beauty of His being.

In the writings of Fredrick Ozanam we come across this profound observation:

> There exists at the bottom of human nature an imperishable paganism which wakes up in every century, which is not dead in ours, and which is always ready to fall back into pagan philosophies, into pagan laws, pagan arts, because men find therein the realization of their

dreams and the satisfaction of their instincts. Greece deified strength, riches, pleasure.

To properly estimate our own days, we have to call these words to mind, since if we do, we will no longer be surprsied at the thoughts and activities of those of our own day, since we will realize that we live in a neo-pagan society and in which society the Church of Rome stands up for the values that have dominated the lives of the great men and women who had the grace to live in that age opposed to our own and in which Christian principles were the dominating force. Along with the words of Fredrick Ozanam, we have those of St. Peter Canisius, who writes this of his own day:

> We have the bitter experience of the difficulties of our own generation and know the appalling changes to which everything is subject, as if the world was in its last delirium and about to collapse into nothingness. There is no place of rest for us except in the wounds of our crucified Lord—in them is our home, our harbor, our sanctuary. Let the world indulge in its madness. Let it wear itself out...it is growing old. I think it is in its last decrepit state.
> (from the *Life of St. Peter Canisius* by James Broderick, S.J.)

It is when we have the grace to read words like these we thank God for the gift of faith in the holy Roman Catholic Church, since it is in Her alone that can be had the "home," the "harbor" and the "sanctuary" of which St. Peter Canisius speaks to us, as well as does the psalmist in the opening words of the ninety-first psalm, seeing we there read:

> You who dwell in the shelter of the Most High,
> Who abide in the shadow of the almighty.
> Say to the Lord, "My refuge and my fortress,
> My God, in whom I trust."
> For he will rescue me from the snare of the fowler,
>   from the destroying pestilence.
> With his pinions he will cover you,
> and under his wings you shall take refuge.

One has to beg forgiveness for making such a long quote. But as we read these lines are not we reminded of the protection we receive from the falsehoods and errors of our own day, which the Church of Rome provides for us in a spiritual and intellectual way? I for one, and with me all the saints and those among them known as the Fathers and Doctors of the Church, have always held that the "words of Moses are the words of Christ," and that not only are the words of Moses alone the words of Christ, but those also spoken by all the prophets, chief among these being the "sweet singer of Israel," as the Holy Spirit designates the author of at least half of the book of psalms, namely the Jewish King David. It is of the Church of Rome the psalmist sings in these sublime hymns, so it is for this reason she, the Church of Rome, has always taken these songs close to her heart and made them the chief words with which to send up praise to Almighty God.

It is to the Church of Rome the psalmist has reference when he tells us that those "who dwell in the shadow of the Almighty" are none other than are the members of the Mystical Body of Christ, seeing they will in that way be rescued and sheltered from the snare of the fowler Satan will always be. It is to the Church of Rome we must go if we wish to have the kind of security to be had in no other religious institution on this earth today. It is not to Judaism or any of the many other religions in the world we must go for the "rest of the mind" and for the "peace of heart" of which Fredrick Ozanam speaks when he tells us that he has known the difficulties of belief of his own day, but that his "whole life has taught him that there is neither rest for the mind nor peace for the heart save in the Church and in obedience to her authority."

I sometimes wonder if those who read this biography will wonder at my making so many quotes from the writings of the saints in the place of my own words. To this, can be replied the words of St. Augustine in which he said he would rather read what others had written than do his own writing, and I have always agreed with him along this line. I too would much rather read the writings of the saints than do my own writing, and I have read the writings of the saints throughout the fifty-two years of my life as a Catholic, and it is due to this kind of reading that whatever good things I have the grace to have, have been acquired. They have been acquired by reading all the saints have written about the truths of our holy Roman Catholic faith.

We can no more imagine a world without the Church in it than we can think of the sun being taken from the sky, and we find Fredrick Ozanam saying these words in reference to the religion we have the grace to believe: "The grandeur of Catholicism!" How many Catholics have the same estimable view of the Church of Rome? All the saints did. They all said these things of her: "Ah, you are beautiful, my beloved.... Ah, you are beautiful...yes, you are lovely"(Canticle of Canticles 1:15). It is of the Church of Rome these words have been spoken by the Holy Spirit, the Church of Rome being as she is the Mystical Body of Him who forms one Person with her, so that what we say of Christ is equally attributed to her whose mystical Bride she is.

"Yes, you are lovely," we say in reference to the Church of Rome, and I as a convert to her, can never cease exalting her sublime being. The Church has made me the person I am so how can I stop expressing my gratitude to her that out of a confused person spiritually and intellectually, I am now by the grace of God one of the most peaceful human beings who walks this earth, and I would no more exchange the riches of heaven's gifts the truths of faith have conferred on me than would a grown up person exchange the Empire State Building for the little toy house cherished by a baby. Besides, aren't all the monstrous sky structures of our big cities nothing but the toys of little children? Aren't they all nothing but the mud houses children make to amuse themselves with?

To get back to the story of my conversion to the holy Roman Catholic faith—how can I ever stop extolling the beauty of that faith and cease calling that faith by sweet and holy names! I cannot do so, because that which I now do in an imperfect way, will be the occupation I shall have in heaven. I shall there thank God for the grace of being able to believe in all that the Church teaches, and to glory in that faith and in those teachings—did not St. Teresa of Avila say these words on her way out of this world, and may it be my grace to speak the same words on my way out of this world: "After all I am a daughter of the Church," words which constituted her admission ticket to eternal happiness. And, while the world God has made has many things to offer us by way of good and beautiful in it, she cannot give us eternal life, the kind of eternal life Christ came on earth to bring and which same it is the express desire of Almighty God that the Church promulgates, and this even at the cost of suffering and persecution to herself. Have not millions upon millions had the grace to lay down their lives in defense of the truths of faith? Where would we today be but for the blood of the martyrs which is the "seed of the faith"? I often call to mind the price that has already been paid for the consolations I now receive in being able to believe in all that the Church teaches, the price beginning with the sufferings of the Cross, and the carrying of these sufferings and even deaths by millions who, like Christ, have received the grace to die for the things they held more precious than life itself.

"In your fight against sin you have not yet resisted to the point of shedding blood" (Heb. 12:14) St. Paul reminds us. We must ask for the grace to think of these words when some inconvenience and discomfort arises in our lives in connection with the practice of our holy Catholic religion, for we have not yet resisted to the point of shedding blood because of our belief in the holy Roman Catholic Church, though that time may come in our lives, seeing the whole world has risen up against the truths of faith and that with the psalmist, those who harbor animosity against the Church of Rome say,

> Why do the nations rage
> and the people utter vain folly?
> The kings of the earth rise up,
> and the princes conspire together
> Against the lord and against his anointed
> Let us break their fetters
> and cast their bonds from us.
> (Ps. 2:1-3)

It is of the Church of Rome these words are written. It is against her, "kings of the earth rise up, and the princes conspire together."

One can go on and on in this way, and quote passage after passage from the Holy Scripture to point out that the Church of Rome will always have to undergo persecution at the hand of those who harbor animosity against her holy teachings, for it is really the devil himself who will always be behind these persecutions, even as it was the devil who put it into the heart of Judas to betray Christ. And so, with all this before us, we who have the grace to love the Church as the mother of our spiritual and intellectual life, it is our privileged task to extol our holy Mother Church and to lavish on her the love of our whole hearts, so that with the words of the Song of Songs we should say in reference to all that she is, namely the Bride of Christ, "Ah, you are beautiful, my beloved.... Ah, you are beautiful...yes, you are lovely" and when our time arrives for us to leave this world we should receive the grace to say, "After all, I am a daughter of the Church," as well as to repeat the above beautiful words of the Song of Songs in reference to her sublime and exalted being, for sublime and exalted her being is, seeing she has opened for us the path leading to the joys we shall experience as soon as we close our eyes in death. As soon as we close our eyes in death, we shall be in the paradise of God and rejoice with Him in His eternal glory. For, in heaven, Christ's glory will be our glory, and his joys will there become our very own. Amen.

* * *

Many years ago, a professor of English literature said these words to me:

> There are two kinds of people in the Church who write. One of these writes because he or she is a professional writer, while there are others who write because they pray. Now, you [meaning me] are not a professional writer and you never will be one. You write because you pray; don't write unless you pray.

The reason these words were spoken to me was that this professor knew I had not received a formal education, having arrived in the United States at the age of ten. I went three years to a public school, but at age thirteen, may father had me obtain working papers because the family was so destitute. I worked for about three or four years and after that as I have previously written, gave up most of my time to improve myself along educational lines.

Now, why do I bring all this up in the course of writing down my thoughts in this autobiography? I do this because every now and then, as I go on writing, I reach a point where I wonder if I should go on writing or stop at the point I had reached doing so, and this because as I have already mentioned, with St. Augustine I'd rather read what others have written than to do my own writing. Still, there are the eighty-five years of my life which is God's greatest gift and there is need to be grateful for such a gift, so at the advice of my professor friend, I pray to know what further things to say.

As I said in the beginning, it was fifty-two years ago, when some of my best friends then suggested I should write the story of my conversion to the Catholic faith, and every time I tried to do this, I became very distracted by the effort I made, so that I could not center my heart and mind on the things eternal which are matters for prayer. And so, fifty-two years later, I said to myself, supposing I now try to do what I was then unable to do? So I put a sheet of paper into the typewriter and said a prayer to one of my favorite saints, noted for her literary and religious genius, St. Teresa of Avila, and began writing. An hour or so passes by and I find myself with four or five pages before me. As I re-read them, I wonder how someone like myself, with practically no formal schooling, could have written what's before me, so the only explanation is that someone who has long left this world assisted me doing what with my own ability alone could never have been accomplished. I have read in the *Vida* (Life) written by herself, that St. Teresa had a similar experience and that she too felt that someone else besides herself helped her write what she did, so this was consoling to realize.

Having lived such a long time in this world, a person accumulates a vast amount of spiritual and intellectual riches, so that the problem arises as to whether there is an obligation on that person's part to share these riches with those about him, especially, his friends in Christ. I consulted my spiritual director in this matter, and he left no doubt in my mind that there is an obligation to share with others what one has learned by personal experience, and so this is the reason for my now writing this autobiography, which one of the dearest friends I have on this earth tells me I should not stop writing, and that she would both edit the text and have it published after my death. And so I have to keep on doing what I started out a few months ago, as I do so, the problem arises as to what to select from the thousands of details and incidents which would be of interest to those who will read what has been written. As far as I am concerned, I have since my conversion been interested in one sole thing: how to become more closely united to God by the means provided for such unity by the holy Roman Catholic Church, seeing it is in her alone I find what interests me most in this life, the things of the spirit and how to become a saint, the Catholic Church being a saint-maker, if one is allowed to express himself in this way. It is to enable me to become a saint I got the grace to be able to believe in all that the Church teaches, and if my aim was not to become a saint, I don't think it to be worthwhile to undergo all the trials and tribulations conversion implies. Why be a Catholic for any reason less than to ask God to give us the grace to become saints? Does not Fredrick Ozanam say these words along this line: "Ordinary Catholics are plentiful enough; we need saints." It is to become saints that those outside the Church should ask for the grace to become the members of the Mystical Body of Christ and not just to attain the salvation of one's immortal soul, seeing by becoming saints, we will get the grace to by-pass purgatory and go straight to heaven when we die.

I once walked into a Catholic Church and heard these words from the mouth of a priest in the pulpit: "Everyone in this church tonight is going to go to purgatory." I did not at all like such a dreary remark so I went to see my learned spiritual director and asked him if a person may have a moral certainty of going to heaven without going to purgatory, and he said yes—he of course said this with the implication that such a person would accept the suffering of this life in the place of purgatory, because no one can attain to his beatific state without having undergone the necessary refinement of soul to enter into this beatific state.

As I said, as I keep writing, the problem arises as to what to say, and so for this, one has to have recourse to prayer, and that is what I intend doing right now. So with this in view, I bring this page to a close and wait for God to make His will known as regards to what should be stated in future writings.

*   *   *

I have been asked to write about Christ in this autobiography. But the response to this request has to be that everything in this biography is about Christ and what is not in relationship to Christ should not be in this biography. And for that matter if we read a book and do not find the name of Christ in that book then it will be of no spiritual profit to read such a book. I have already quoted the words of St. Bernard in this matter, and they are worth quoting again: "If thou writest, thy composition has no charm for me, unless I read there the name of Jesus" (Sermon XIII on the Canticle of Canticles). Is it not Jesus we need in our lives if these lives are to be what it is God's will for them to be? I once asked the father of a little boy what he thought of his son, and this is the answer he gave: "He is my whole life." Up to a point, what this father said was true; but up to a certain point these words should apply to Christ the Lord; He it is who should be our "whole life." It is to Christ St. Francis of Assisi has reference when he said: "My God and my All." Christ should be All to us. He was All to the saints. The saints had no problems because their problems were solved by their faith in Christ. "God is all; man is nothing," a great Jewish convert, the Ven. Mary Paul Libermann said as he lay dying. I repeat these words and say with them that Christ is all and man is nothing, seeing I have since my conversion been unable to think of God save in the Person of His Son, and is this not a blessed impossibility! I shall go further and affirm I have not been able to think of the Person of Christ without at the same time calling to mind the Blessed Virgin Mary.

And so when I am asked to write more about Christ, I repeat the words of St. Bernard and say with him what he says in reference to Christ. When I think of God, the Holy Name of Jesus is never absent from my mind and heart. Christ is all to me, because what He is not, is nothing to me. It is hard to think of Christ because it is hard to speak of God, being that He is infinite goodness, infinite truth and infinite beauty. But fortunately for us, this infinity of goodness, truth and beauty became flesh so that we may in that way get a living experience of the Majesty of the Divine Being.

When I first came to the United States, we lived in a neighborhood that had a Protestant missionary store with these words in the window of that store: "God so loved the world that He gave

His Only-Begotten Son," etc. I was then around ten years old and so every time I passed by this window and read these words I was puzzled. With my Jewish mentality, I felt God could not be spoken of in that way, but I could never stop thinking of these words. So how grateful to God I now am for that impossibility, yes, a million thousand times. So what the father of the little boy said of his son, I say of Christ: "He is my whole life." How I thank God for being able to say such words: "Thou shalt love the Lord thy God with thy whole heart, with thy whole mind and with all thy strength." Every time I say these words I say, "Thou shalt love the Lord Christ," etc. How sorry I shall always feel for the Jewish people for their not being able to love the Holy Name of Jesus and experience what St. Bernard has written about that Name: "Jesus is honey in the mouth, melody in the ear, jubilation in the heart" (Sermon XIII on the Canticle of Canticles). Yes, Jesus is "honey" in the spiritual and intellectual way that that word implies. How sad it is to see so many devoid of grace to believe in Christ and with that belief get a taste on earth of what the joys of heaven are like. Is it not what the joy of the psalmist has in view when he says "Taste and see how good [Hebrew: "sweet"] the Lord is"? It most certainly is, because St. Augustine says it is of Christ the Lord the psalmist speaks, when he tells us he "heard the voice of Christ in the psalms."

Christ is everything to me. What He is not, is nothing. It is Him I have the grace to detect in the soul of every person I meet. He exists in that person in a marvellously sweet way. "Do you not know that Jesus is in you," St. Paul says to those about him. And does not St. John of the Cross tell us that "beside this life of love through which the soul that loves God lives in Him, her life is radically and naturally centered in God, like all created things, centered in God, as St. Paul says, 'In him we live, move and are ' " (*Spiritual Canticle*, Stanza 8).

Someone who has the grace to be as close to God as anyone I have ever met, and whose whole being is centered around Christ the Lord, has asked me to write down my personal views and even experiences of the beauty of Christ, as she put it. But how write about the beauty that's infinite in extent and has no limits set to its nature and essence? "My heart has uttered a good matter," the psalmist says in his opening word in which the beauty of Christ is spoken of. "I declare my works to the king: my tongue is the pen of a quick writer. Thou [meaning Christ] art more beautiful than the sons of men: grace has been shed forth on thy lips: therefore God has blessed thee forever. Gird thy sword upon thy thigh, O mighty One, in thy comeliness, and in thy beauty" (Ps. 44(45):1-2, Septuagint Version).

I quote these words because it is the oldest translation of the psalms in existence, so the original Hebrew text from which this translation has been made may be more accurate than the one we have today of the Hebrew text. Anyway, it is because direct reference is here made to the beauty of Christ's Being which makes these words particularly appealing to me. I have always seen in them reference to the personal beauty of Christ's Being. Also, because I remember reading St. Robert Bellarmine saying that there are many things about the life of Christ that are not treated of in the four Gospels because they're recorded in the Book of Psalms, so it is to them, as well as to the other parts of the Scriptures we must go for a more complete description of all our Lord was when He assumed our human nature. Along this line, who does not recall the beautiful words that are written of Christ in the Song of Songs? Do we not there read the following words in that Song spoken of Christ: "Ah, you are beautiful, my lover—yes, you are lovely. . . . Ah, you are beautiful, my beloved, ah, you are beautiful!" (Song 1:15, 4:1). Do we not here have the most clear-cut and direct reference to the beauty of Christ's Being, and is it not Him the author of the Song of Songs has in view when he was inspired to write down the words which the Holy Spirit has Himself inspired him to write? And, did not the entire Jewish tradition refer these words to the Messiah for whose coming the Jewish people had prayed during the many centuries prior to the Incarnation?

History records that prior to the fourteenth century the Song of Songs has, with few exceptions, been interpreted in an allegorical way, and it was only with the coming of Protestantism that this kind of interpretation was abandoned for the literal one. I go into all this for the very simple reason that we have in the Song of Songs God's own view of the beauty of Christ's

Being, and that this beauty is there spoken of in figurative terms. What matters though is that it is the beauty of Christ that this Song speaks and it is to this Song I have always gone for a detailed description of the beauty of Him I have the grace to now love more than I do anything else God has made, including my own self.

And so, if my dear saintly friend wishes to know what the beauty of Christ was like, let her turn to the source I have always gone to for this kind of knowledge, but let her read what is there spoken of Christ's beauty in a mystical and figurative way, since read in this way, a new world is opened up to the soul's inner vision, it there discerns what is purely heavenly and divine, and what is purely ineffable in nature and all of which the Person of Our Lord is.

Yes, "Thou art more beautiful than the sons of men," we repeat with the divine psalmist, so it is to the words the psalmist writes of Christ we must go to get a living experience of what the beauty of Christ's Being is. And is it not to the words of the psalmist all the saints have gone for a living experience of the beauty of Christ's Being? Did not St. Teresa of Avila do this when she speaks of the "whiteness of Christ's hands" she received in a vision of Him? Along with her, do we not find St. Gertrude the Great telling us of an experience of the beauty of Christ's Being in the following words:

> Being, then, in the middle of our dormitory...I beheld Thee, my most loving Love and my Redeemer, surpassing in beauty the children of men, under the form of a youth of sixteen years, beautiful and amiable and attracting my heart and eyes.
> (*Revelations of St. Gertrude*, Book 2)

Every saint has a similar experience though in a different way. They all had a vision of the beauty of Christ's Being and fell in love with that beauty so that they could never again become captivated by any created thing, be that beautiful as it may. It was for Christ's beauty the saints longed and not for that of any other human being and this no matter how beautiful that human being may be.

There is a story told of Thomas Isaac Hecker—he has himself

narrated this story. He said that he was seated on his bed one day and there came to him a beautiful figure. He was fully conscious when this experience came to him, and after seeing the beauty of this figure he decided never to get married. He felt he would never find a woman as beautiful as this figure was. Many saints were led away from the love of created beauty by the visions they received of the beauty of the celestial figures and it was as the result of these visions they could never again become enticed by any earthly beauty.

Well I hope my holy friend will be satisfied with what I just have written concerning the beauty, the ineffable beauty of Christ's Being, and of which same ineffable beauty all the saints received a living experience and which same living experience was responsible for their becoming the saints they became—including also my own dear saintly friend who had asked I write something about the beauty of Christ. I personally don't think any human being can completely give up his and her love for created beauty unless God has vouchsafed them a living experience of His own beautiful Being in the Person of our Divine Lord.

"Ah, you are beautiful, my beloved....Ah, you are beautiful, my lover, yes, you are lovely." More beautifully of Christ no one has ever spoken. The more real and the more vivid Jesus becomes in my life, the less real and the less vivid everything He is not, becomes. Had not this become the case that with St. Teresa—I feel those in heaven to be real to me and it is among them I "live and move and have my being" (Acts 17:28)? There is too much of the physical and what is material in the thought of men and the realization of this depresses the soul. Before I became a Catholic I found the world most men inhabit to be a source of disappointment and dissatisfaction to my way of thinking and feeling, so I took refuge in the writings of the great mystics of the world. How oppressive it is not to be able to breathe the supernatural! How spiritually and intellectually stifling the cast of thought among such a vast number of human beings! How anyone can put up with the miseries of this life without the hope of heaven's joys in his heart, I will only be able to fully understand when I get to heaven. I feel saddened at the thought of so many outside the household of the true faith the Church can alone be for a human being. Take away faith in Christ and I literally could not go on living another minute—the absence of the supernatural world stifles the mind. It would stop the soul's breath.

I write all this to express my gratitude to God for His gift of the Catholic faith to me—a gift with which no other can be compared, including the one my existence is, seeing it would have profited me nothing to have been born if I did not in due time receive the grace to become a Catholic. There is a passage in the book of Ecclesiastes that has puzzled many of its readers, so perhaps when we read that "those now dead, I declared more fortunate in death than are the living to be still alive" (Ecc. 4:2), these words may perhaps in a wide sense be interpreted to signify that without faith in Christ it were better we had never been born, seeing that such a life would be no life at all but the kind of death to which St. Augustine has reference when he refers to this life with the words: "This is the land of the dead." To repeat, it would have profited me nothing to have been born if I did not in due time receive the grace to become a Catholic. With this in view, I will probably spend my eternity thanking God for the gift of faith, a gift, as I said, with which none other can compare, not even the one existence is. Without faith in Christ, we do not even live. Without faith in Christ, we do not live the Life He came to bring.

I know someone reading all this may think it a highly exaggerated form of thinking and feeling. But to me, the exaggerated form of thinking and feeling is to live a life devoid of faith in Christ and the Church founded by Him. It is in being a Catholic that we are really alive in the Christlike sense of that word. It is in being a Catholic, that I feel myself to exist. Without Christ, without the Church of Rome there is nothing but spiritual and intellectual death for me. Without faith in Christ, I do not feel myself to be the human being God wants me to be—I only feel myself to be real in the Reality Christ is.

It is not easy to write the story of one's inner being, seeing that in order to do so we have to lay bare our inmost self for others to see and perceive. It is a kind of nakedness of soul to do so, bringing humiliation with the manifestation of ourselves to the eyes of others.

Still, just as those who have gone before us did not shun the humiliating experience of writing about their own selves, so we today must not shun such an experience, for humiliating it will always be to lay bare our inmost self for others to look at. As I said, and will repeat over and over, I don't see how I personally can go on living without faith in Christ. And, how others can do so, I will only be able to know when I get to heaven, it is there alone I will be able to know how so many were able to endure the miseries of their mortal lot without love for Him who is Love Itself, seeing for me, Christ is everything, and what He is not, is nothing at all. Let the world give to others all it has to offer. Let it shower on them its temporal satisfactions. For me, it is Christ that counts and the life eternal He came to bring. It is so hard to write about what can only be properly understood when we get to heaven: our own selves and those about us, seeing we are all of us living mysteries, completely comprehended by Christ alone. He alone has the true insight into ourselves. When we leave this world we will for the first time know all we have been all the time we have lived on this earth, our true selves which will go on existing forever. We want to die so as to in that way to enter into the fullness of the knowledge of all we blessedly are. It is by dying we will become truly alive, alive, that is, with the Life Itself Christ is. The Life He is will then be our own life, seeing we will become completely merged with His own Being, so that what He is, we will be by the gift of glory conferred on us.

When David Livingstone took ill during his combined work as an explorer and missionary, he was laid on a stretcher. As he lay on it, he said these words: "Life looks different from the angle of the horizontal." When we stand beside the grave of someone we had known for half of a lifetime, we get an entirely different perspective of what we generally consider of great importance. Yesterday I stood beside the grave of someone who had received the grace to dedicate her entire adult life to her love for Christ and the Church He founded. What were some of the thoughts that then came to me? They would be too numerous for words to express. I thought of the many years this person spent at the foot of the altar and the inconceivable joys she now experiences as the result of all the sacrifices she had the grace to make by means of her life as a religious of the Society of the Sacred Heart. Then I thought of the hustle and bustle all about me and how the great majority of mankind wastes its God-given existence in the pursuit of what has no relevance for the kind of life which is alone worthy of the name we give to our present form of existence. I thought of the peace and calm they enjoy who now lie buried near the grave of Mother Fitzgerald of the Society of the Sacred Heart, and as I did so, with what compassion my heart was filled for those who are blind to the eternal values brought into this world by means of the Church in which I received the grace to be incorporated into, and this whole universe took on a shadowy existence—it became as though it had never been and Christ alone was real to me, Christ, and the truths of faith I have the grace to love more than I do my own self. I thought of all this as I stood among these graves and recited the Rosary for the souls of those now interred there. I thought of all this and I became overjoyed with gratitude to God for His having given me the grace to become a Catholic.

Yes, I thought of all this and as I did so I recalled the words of Livingstone when he said that "life looks different from the angle of the horizontal." Life looks different when we stand at the foot of the grave of someone we had known a long time in Christ the Lord. We then think of the soul of that someone which is now in the state of glory, and we envy that soul and we wish we were ourselves in the place of infinite bliss in which that soul has the blessedness to be. How empty and vain this whole world becomes and how utterly insignificant. Yes, we think of all this and as we do so, we repeat the words of the Book of Ecclesiastes and say with the sacred author of that book: "And those now dead, I declared more fortunate in death than are the living to be still alive" (Ecc. 4:2), words which have perplexed the minds of those who comment on them and who have wrongly concluded that the world we are in is a depressing place in which to be, and that there is no meaning to the life of a human being. All these commentators were mistaken in their pessimistic interpretation of these words because for those who love Christ, they are a source of intense delight, seeing they speak to us of the kind of life which shall be our own as soon as we close our eyes in death. The author of the Book of Ecclesiastes envied the dead: he felt sorry for those who while they live, have to remain away from the Infinite Good, Truth and Beauty Jesus is. The sacred writer envies the dead in Christ and he has compassion for those who, being in the state of mortality, are in the words of St. Paul, "away from the Lord" (2 Cor. 5:6). Yes, I thought of all this as I stood by the grave of someone I knew so well in Christ the Lord.

I then thought of heaven and all the inconceivable joys there awaiting us. So I grew saddened at the thought of my not yet being where I will become a participant of these joys and where this soul has the blessedness to now be. As I stood by this grave the whole world took on a different perspective and I was given the grace to feel sorry for those who are enslaved to the goods of time. It is on eternity I then thought and of Christ the Lord, who, St. Bernard says, is eternity. "He, Christ," he says, "is eternity." It is on the Eternity Christ is I thought as I stood beside the grave. I realized how inconceivably happy she is who is now buried in this grave. "Where are your plagues, O death! Where is your sting, O nether world!" (Hos. 13:14). May God be praised for His giving me the grace to know and love Christ and the holy Roman Catholic Church which He founded. Compared with this gift, all the world has to offer is the "rubbish" of which St. Paul speaks when he says, "I have come to rate all as loss in the light of the surpassing knowledge of my Lord Jesus Christ. For his sake I have forfeited everything; I have accounted all else rubbish" (Phil. 3:8).

Of late, it is getting so that when I wake up I feel myself surprised at my still being in this world—there being so little left in me which belongs to time. With St. Realino, I have for a long time already felt that the "earth is not the Christian's home. So let those who want it have the earth." In a way, I was always a Catholic; for, though being raised up in a strong Jewish Hassidic environment, I never felt at home in this world—I identified being a Christian Catholic with not feeling at home in this world, so as I find myself approaching the end of my life, the conviction I have of this world not being my home, reinforces iteslf. Does not he psalmist say "I am a wayfarer [Hebrew: foreigner] on earth?" so as I find myself approaching the end of my life, the conviction I have of this world not being my home, reinforces itself. Does not the psalmist say "I am a wayfarer [Hebrew: foreigner] on earth"?

And does not St. Paul affirm it "we have our citizenship in heaven" and that "we have a dwelling provided for us by God, a dwelling in the heavens, not made by hands but to last forever" (2 Cor. 5:1). With this in view, my not feeling myself at home in this world, Christianity became very congenial to my Jewish mentality, and I am convinced that those who have the grace to be totally oriented to the Catholic way of thinking and feeling have the same experience. No, I never felt completely at home in this world, so I look forward to my now leaving it the way and manner in which all the saints looked forward to their own departure from this life, with a sanctified kind of joy in their hearts—did not one of them say: "I thought I was going to die and my heart nearly broke with joy" (St. Therese).

I have already quoted what I felt to be the most beautiful words ever written on the subject of Christian death. So, if the reader will permit, I will quote them again in their entirety seeing they are written by the greatest Doctor of Mystical Theology the Church has produced, St. John of the Cross:

> The soul does nothing very outstanding by wanting to die at the sight of the beauty of God in order to enjoy Him forever. Were she to have but a foreglimpse of the height and beauty of God, she would not only desire death in order to see Him now forever, as she here desires, but she would very gladly undergo a thousand singularly bitter deaths to see Him only for moment; and having seen Him, she would ask to suffer just as many more that she might see Him for another moment.
>
> (*Spiritual Canticle*, Stanza II)

And just as St. John of the Cross has written more profoundly and more sublimely on the transformation of the soul in Christ, so he has written the most beautiful words on the subject of a holy and a happy death. So much so is this the case, that when we read what he has to say along these lines, we recall the words of the book of Ecclesiastes and say with the author of them, "And those now dead, I declared more fortunate in death than are the living to be still alive" (Ecclesiastes 4:2).

And so, as I feel myself waking up in the morning, I get really surprised to still find myself in this world and my not yet having gone from it. With Pope John XXIII I say that my "bags" are not only "packed", but I am like a person at the railroad station who is waiting for the train to arrive which will take him to the destination he has for years been looking forward to get to. I have for years been looking forward to going home to God in His high heaven, so this is the reason I cannot understand why I have been kept away from my home for such a long time. When I became a Catholic, I said these words to myself: "The doors of heaven have been opened up for me—they did so with my baptism—so why remain on this earth?" I felt there was a reason for my remaining in this world before I became a Catholic, but that now, with the gift of faith in a life infinitely more beautiful than this, why not go to that life by means of a holy and happy death, seeing it is by this means we are made completely one with our divine Lord, so that what He is by Nature, we become by means of grace and glory. And so, it is for this reason when I wake up in the morning I feel myself surprised for being still in time and not in God's holy Eternity. "Ich liebe dich O weig keit" (I love thee, O eternity!) I say with the arch-enemy of the Christian religion (Friedrich Nietzsche), but I say these words for an entirely different reason. I say these words because for a Christian, by the word eternity Christ is indicated, seeing that St. Bernard tells us that "He, Christ, is eternity." And so, it is in view of all this that I repeat the words of St. Realino and say with him that "Earth is not the Christian's home. Let those who want it have the earth." Let those have what the world has to offer who are devoid of faith in Christ. They who have the grace to have such faith say "Vanity of vanities...vanity of vanities! All things are vanity," (Ecclesiastes 1:1) and by "vanity" is signified the mere breath of air all created things are compared with the invisible things of Almighty God and which same are laid up for us in the life to come. It is for that life it is God's will we should yearn and long with our whole hearts, with our whole minds and with our whole might, seeing it is for that life we have been made by an infinitely loving Lord. We have not been created for the few paltry years of the present life. We have been put on this earth so that we may have the grace to long for what will never have an end with time. We have been born so that we may in that way be made ineffably one with our divine Lord Jesus Christ.

When the Jewish convert, the Venerable Mary Paul Libermann, would feel discouraged he said these words to himself: "I am a Christian, I am a Christian," and if they were supernaturally wise in Christ the Lord, every Jewish convert should say these words to him and herself, myself included. And just as St. Teresa used to cheer herself up with the words, "After all, I am a daughter of the Church," every Jewish convert should repeat the words of the Ven. Libermann and say with him "I am a Christian, I am a Christian," or, better still, "I am a Catholic," seeing if he or she did so, they would experience a delight from heaven with which no merely human joy can compare.

Yes, I am a Catholic, I so often say to myself in an inward way, and without the noise of words of any kind, and feeling myself to be one reminds me of the words of Fredrick Ozanam in which he asserts the following: "The experience of my whole life has taught me that there is neither rest for the mind nor peace for the heart save in the holy Roman Catholic Church and in obedience to her authority." And should I be devoid of the grace to repeat these words, I could not go on living another minute nor would I want to do so even if I could live on in this life. And so for me, it is either the Church of Rome or no existence in time, seeing one without the other is inconceivable. I cannot imagine how a person can go on living without faith in Christ and the Church He founded and I thank God for my not being able to do so.

Every human being glorifies God. He does so by the mere fact of his having been born into this world, and so he should for this reason leave a record behind as to who he had been all the time he was on this earth. But, for the majority of mankind, this is an ideal only so they will have to wait for this ideal to be realized when they get to heaven where they will glorify God by thanking Him for His having given them their existence in time—they will do this with that part of themselves made in the image of Christ. With the Psalmist he will all say "I give you thanks that I am fearfully [Hebrew: awesomely, reverentially], wonderfully made" (Ps. 138:14).

There will always be those who get the great grace to glorify God in the present life, and they will do this by the paintings they make, by the poetry they write and by the music they compose. They will also accomplish this glorification of Christ by the plain prose they write, and this is something God has given even myself to do. I have for years felt that before we leave this world we should ask for the grace to leave behind a record of all we have been from a spiritual and intellectual point of view, so that those who come after us will know what in the eyes of God we have been. I said that such glorification of Christ the Lord is for the majority of the human race an ideal to be realized in the next life, though for a select few there is given the grace for them to glorify God before they get to heaven. I have in the beginning of this narrative, singled out three such great men and one woman, beginning with St. Augustine in his *Confessions,* St. Teresa in her *Life* and Cardinal Newman in his *Apologia Pro Vita Sua.* In between these three spiritual giants there are numberless records of the lives of other human beings among whom I have in all humility been given the grace to be included. I have in the beginning of this biography quoted the opening words of *Paradise Lost,* and said with Milton

I thence
Invoke thy aid to my adventurous Song
That with no middle flight intends to soar.

I appended these words on the first page of this biography, because I too "with no middle flight" intend to glorify God for all He has done for me ever since I am able to remember. He has done this by placing me in the company of devout Hassidic Jewish men who remained unmarried so that they could in that way give themselves entirely up to prayer and the study of the Holy Scriptures; therefore, I have always felt the need for giving thanks to God by means of the written word. I have always felt that I owed God a debt which can only be fully paid Him in the next life, and only in a limited degree while we are not yet completely with Him in the world to come. I have always felt that not only I myself owe God such a debt, but that every single human being owes Him such a debt, and for most men this debt will be paid when they meet God in the face-to-face vision of His Infinite Beauty. And while it would certainly be a wonderful thing if every human being born into this world received the grace to leave behind a written account of all he had been in an intellectual and spiritual way, it remains for the few to be able to do this. And so for those who are able to leave behind a record of all they had been while they were on this earth, for those few an obligation exists which they cannot evade. They cannot evade the obligation of thanking God for the existence they have, as well as to leave behind for others to read a written account of their existence and which same so many have had the grace to do, seeing it is given to every human being to repeat the words of the psalmist and with him say to God, "I give you thanks that I am fearfully, wonderfully made."

Yes, we must thank God for all we have received from Him in a physical and spiritual way—body and soul, we are obliged to Him for everything we have and are and we glorify Him for the existence we have and we do so by means of the written word. Many have already done so; so it but remains for us as well to add to their list of praises and thanksgiving for the grace to find ourselves in the present life. All the time we find ourselves in the present life, something wonderfully and ineffably divine is taking place, and it is too holily sublime for human expression. We must make an effort to say this to God and this no matter how imperfectly we are able to do this in a literary way. Yes, all of us should say to God, "I give you thanks that I am fearfully, wonderfully made" because we would in this way glorify God in His divine Son in whose image we have been made. It is His image in us which makes us pleasing to our Father in heaven and His image alone. It is during our lifetime we should praise God so that we may receive the reward of this praise when we get to heaven.

After two hundred pages, it should not be surprising if the autobiography has reached a dilemma. Should this narrative continue being expanded with details and reminiscences of a spiritual and intellectual life which continues on existing long after the body has disintegrated in the grave? For one may ask, what is the real life of a human being and is that life restricted to the part of himself he has in common with the lower animals? In short, what is the real me? Is it not that part of myself made in the image and likeness of God and in which we resemble the holy angels? In assessing our own being, we must distinguish beween what we ourselves are and what belongs to us, for that is the real person which keeps on existing after we leave this world, namely, the spiritual and intellectual part of ourselves and not what we have in common with the rest of creation, and it is about real part of ourselves has taken flight to its home in heaven, where that part of ourselves was conceived and created and later on deposited in our mother's womb. It is about the part of ourselves made in God's image we should write and not on what is accidental and temporal in our makeup, since that is our real selves which shall go on existing for all eternity and that in ourselves which shall not go on existing for all eternity is in the eyes of God nothing at all so that part of ourselves is not at all worth writing about and to leave a record behind.

Along this line, does not St. Paul say to us the following words:

> I have been crucified with Christ, and the life I live now is not my own; Christ is living in me. I still live my human life, but it is a life of faith in the Son of God, who loved me and gave himself for me. (Gal. 2:20)

It is this life in us which Christ is which should be so termed and not that in ourselves Christ is not. It is Christ in ourselves which constitutes God's image, seeing it is in His image we have been made and it is this image of Christ in ourselves which distinguishes us from the lower animals. What we have in common with the lower animals belongs to us and it is not we ourselves; what we ourselves are is made in the image of Christ so that part of ourselves belongs to Him and it is for that part of ourselves our Lord gave His life to redeem. And so, as I keep writing this biography, I have in view that part of myself in which I resemble God and no other part of my being. It is not the mortal part of myself it is my intention to here record, but that in myself which shall go on existing without any end to that existence. It is about the spiritual and intellectual part of myself I feel I should write, seeing that that is the real me, and not what has to have an end with time. It is not what's laid in the grave that constitutes our real and our true selves but that only which, after it has left its earthly habitation, takes its flight to its home in heaven. It is the immortal soul in a human being which consitutes his real self so it is about that part of him which is alone worth making a record of for others to read.

Many people never get to know their real selves because they never get to know Christ who alone constitutes the real self in them. And this is a tragedy of the first order. It is nothing sad that we have to leave this world—what's so pathetic is that many leave this world who never got to know and to love that in themselves in which they resemble the holy angels. Many never get to know Christ and never getting to know Him, they remain in ignorance of that in themselves which is alone worth knowing and loving. Along this line, has not someone said is it not the soul the soul loves in another human being? It is, because it is that alone, his soul that is alone worthy of our knowledge and the love we should have proportionate to that knowledge, "the life I live now is not my own: Christ is living in me," are the words we should repeat with the apostle to the Gentiles.

No it is not what we have in common with the lower animals which constitutes our real and true selves—what we have in common with the lower animals will one day be laid in the grave and so it does not for this reason constitute the selves for which Christ laid down His precious Life. And so it is about that part of myself it is the aim to say something about which has a relevance for the life to come. What has no relevance for the life to come, is in the eyes of God nothing at all, and so it is not worth writing about. What is worth writing about is that in ourselves we have in common with the holy angels and with them alone. What we have in common with the lower animals does not constitute our true and real selves and so it is not worth writing about.

The question can be asked as follows: What is it I love when I love someone like my own self? Do I love the animal part of that human being and that in his and her makeup which he or she has in common with the lower animals? Because that, the animals themselves love in each other. What I love when I love another human being is that in that human being made in the image and likeness of Christ, that and no other thing since there is nothing else about a human being worth loving. And not only is the love I have for a human being restricted to that in himself we have in common with the holy angels, namely, his immortal soul, but I don't even love anything in my own self, save that in my own self made in God's image, seeing there is nothing in my own self worth loving save this image of His. It is Christ I love in my own self and it is Him I love in all those whom I love. It is the soul of another person that the soul loves, this and no other thing, seeing it is the soul alone which constitutes the true and real self of a human being and which same alone goes on existing after this life is over. After this life is over, it is the true and real self that will go on existing and nothing else in ourselves in which we did not resemble Christ the Lord. He it is in us, who blessedly constitutes our true and real selves and what He is not in His essential Self is nothing at all and therefore not worth writing about. If we do write about our own selves let it be about that part of ourselves we have in common with the angels and saints in the paradise of God. What is it I love in those I love? I love that part in those I love which shall go on existing for all eternity. What shall not go on existing for all eternity is not worthy of the love and affection of a rational human being.

In a mystical way, which cannot be described, I sometimes see all heaven opened up to my soul's inner sight, and yet I cannot enter into it on account of that part of myself which belongs to my mortal state. When this takes place, I feel with St. Teresa that "I die because I do not die." And this kind of feeling is now acquiring permanence in the state of my soul, so it seems as if I am already three fourths out of this world so I wonder why the rest of myself can endure being deprived of the vision of Christ, and being with Him in the state of glory. During the early years of my life in the Church, I actually prayed for death, my spiritual director having given me permission to do so. But now I just ask for the grace to adjust my own will with God's will, or better still, to make God's will my will and to have no will of my own in this matter. Still, I live in the expectancy of death all the time and the concerns of this world no longer have the slightest interest to me, no more than they do those who are now in the place of infinite bliss, though I do pray for those in the world who along this line have views similar to my own. God has given me the kind of friends who are more angelic than human and I live with the thought of them never absent from my inner being.

Yes, with many of the saints, if not all of them, I find it a trial to go on living, especially now with heaven's joys so deep in my heart.

How anyone can go on living after having had a personal

experience of how good God is, I shall never completely know until I get to heaven. It sometimes even now seems that in a mystical way, that part of myself made in God's image, is already in heaven, and so I am grateful for that taste of the Lord of which the psalmist speaks when he says "Taste and see how good [Hebrew: sweet] the Lord is" (Ps. 34:9). It is now the sunset of my life and I have longed for the sunrise fifty-two years ago, when I received the grace to become a Catholic. I feel that now that I have become a Catholic, the gates of heaven have opened up for me, so why stay on this sad earth? Now, fifty-two years later, I know God had other designs in my regard so I pray for the grace to adjust myself to these designs of His, knowing that whatever is allowed to happen has the good of my soul in view. Still, as I said, with heaven's joys now so deeply rooted in my inner being, it is a trial not to be where these joys can be had in all their fullness in the life to come. But I am in no way distressed by all this because at my age one cannot figure on staying too long in this life. Along this line, does not St. Thomas More tell us that although "we know that a young man may die soon, it is certain an old man can't live long," and it is this certainty which is now such a source of consolation to me. Let those wish to live a long time in this world who have not received a personal experience of what the joys of heaven are like seeing if they had received such an experience they would with all the saints find it a trial to go on living where these joys cannot be had in all their fullness but only by means of a slight taste or the "sip" of them of which St. Teresa speaks.

And so, as I still find myself in the present life, I thank God for every minute of it, fully realizing that ever minute I remain in it, I can glorify God in my desire to be with Him in the state of glory, so that with St. Paul I say the following words:

> Therefore, we continue to be confident. We know that while we dwell in the body we are away from the Lord. We walk by faith, not by sight. I repeat, we are full of confidence and would much rather be away from the body and be at home with the Lord. This being so, we make it our aim to please him whether we are with him or away from him.
> (2 Cor. 5:6-9)

I wake up every morning thanking God that I am a Catholic. If more Catholics did the same thing there would be more joy of heart in the members of Christ's Mystical Body. For just as we take for granted the light of the sun and all the rest of God's natural gifts, so do we take for granted the spiritual gifts of Faith, Hope and Charity, gifts without the possession of which, we would not be the men and women it is God's holy will we should be, that is joyous and happy to a degree unknown by those not blessed with the gift of faith in the holy Roman Catholic Church. A lot of people take pride in the possession of this world's goods. The saint is proud to be the follower of the God-Man and to have the grace to live the Life He lived all the time He walked among men. It is of Christ the saint boasts. It is him he considers his wealth and his glory. For the saints, heaven begins on this earth. They have experience of its joys during the present life. The saints do not have to wait for death to know by personal experience what the joys of heaven are like: they avail themselves of these joys by being members of the household of the true faith Catholicism will always be for those who have eyes to see and ears to hear. The saints are in possession of a vision they experience who are now in heaven. I think of this every time I wake up in the morning. As I do this, I become aware of the inconceivable bliss that is mine in being able to believe in all the truths the Church teaches. Compared to the gift of faith in the holy Roman Catholic Church, all the wealth of the world is nothing but the "rubbish" of which St. Paul speaks when he says to us,

> But those things I used to consider gain I have now reappraised as loss in the light of Christ. I have come to rate all as loss in the light of the surpassing knowledge of my Lord Jesus Christ. For his sake I have forfeited everything; I have accounted all else rubbish so that Christ may be my wealth. . . .
> (Phil. 3:7-8)

The psalmist tells us that we should "shout joyfully" at the realization of the goodness of God to us, the goodness of God made manifest in the gift of faith in all that the Church teaches as regards all that is awaiting us in the life to come. With St. Realino, the saints say that "Earth is not the Christian's home. Let those who want it have the earth." And St. Ignatius Loyola tells us that every time he looked at the heavens he was over-come with contempt for all earthly good things. I think of all this when I wake up in the morning and I realize how blessed by God to have the grace of belonging to the only true Church—Catholicism constituting the joy of heart they experience who are now in heaven. The great German poet Heinrich Heine said that his baptism was his passport to European culture (he was a Jewish convert to Christianity). With Heine, I myself say that my own baptism was the passport to the kind of joys they experience who are now in heaven, my faith in Catholicism giving me a goodly taste of those joys right here on this earth. We are told by the psalmist to "sing to the Lord a new song" (Ps. 33:3) the "new song" Christianity is.

It is this "new Song" I have the grace to sing for the past fifty-two years I have been in the Church. For the fifty-two years I have been in the Church, there has been nothing but singing and music in my heart, the song and music Catholic Christianity will always be for those blessed with the gift of the true faith. "But, I am a Christian, I am a Christian," I say with the great Jewish convert the Venerable Mary Paul Libermann every time I feel tempted to grow sad and despondent at the restrictions of my earthly lot. It is the Most Holy Name of Jesus I then get the grace to pronounce with devotion and love.

Yes, "sing to the Lord a new Song," I say with the psalmist—we sing to the Lord the "new Song" Catholicism is, a song which rejoices the heart with the wine from heaven, intoxicating it with love for Christ. We sing to the Lord the new Song the Church of Rome will always be for those who have been given the grace to cherish Her in their hearts. Is she not meant to be the Mother of our spiritual and intellectual life? Has it not been said that "God is more of a Mother to us than a Father"?

> Near the cross of Jesus there stood His Mother.... Seeing His Mother there with the disciple whom He loved, Jesus said to his mother, "Woman, there is your Son." In turn he said to the disciple, "There is your mother".
> (John 19:25-26)

"Here is your mother," our Lord says as regards the Church of

Rome, for although these words were spoken of the Blessed Virgin Mary, the Church is included in this remark.

We will find Jesus in the Church. He is present in her to a degree we will find Him nowhere else. Does not the Church herself assure us of this in everything written by her since the first day our Lord has said to St. Peter the words, "On this rock I will build my Church"? We re told in the psalms to "Sing to the Lord a new Song," and with the help of God's grace I have been singing this "new Song" to the Lord since the very first day I became a Catholic and I shall continue singing this "Song" to Him for all eternity. How few there are who sing the Song Christ is deep in their inner being, so may I have the grace to be included in these few. As I said, in something I wrote the other day, I wake up in the morning thanking God that I am a Catholic, and I don't see how there is anyone in this world with the gift of faith who should fail to do so, seeing what is there a human being can have in this life to console him the way he can find comfort in the thought of his one day being completely with Christ in the state of glory? What is there a human being can have in this life that equals the joy of heart having such a hope in his inner being, and it is this hope the Church alone can cause us to have. And so, realizing this, how can anyone fail to be overwhelmed with love for Christ in the possession of all the Church assures us we shall possess as soon as we close our eyes in death. And although, I know full well I quoted the following words before, it will be no imposition on those with love for Christ in their hearts to reread them over and over and this on account of the sublimity they contain—has not my learned and holy Jesuit director once said to me these words as regards the writings of St. John of the Cross: "There is nothing more sublime outside the Scriptures" and being sublime the following words cannot be read often enough:

> The soul does nothing very outstanding by wanting to die at the sight of the beauty of God in order to enjoy forever. Were she to have but a foreglimpse of the height and beauty of God, she would not only desire death in order to see Him now forever, as she here desires, but she would very gladly undergo a thousand singularly bitter deaths to see Him only for moment; and having seen Him, she would ask to suffer just as many more that she might see Him for another moment.
> (*Spiritual Canticle* 11:7)

And so, with these words of the Doctor of Mystical Theology deep in our inner being, who can fail to be thankful to God for His gift to him and her for the gift of faith in the only true Church? And although we cannot, with Vatican II, say often enough that the truths of God can be to a limited degree found outside the Church as well, and in all the other religions of the world, it is only in the Church or Rome that these truths can be had in all their fullness and in all their riches, and it is in the realization of this in which the whole of our earthly happiness lies, it does so in no other things to be had on this earth. We have been put on this earth in order that we may realize that it is to the Church of Rome we must go to find all they possess who are now in the state of glory.

And so, realizing all of this, when I wake up every morning the first thought that comes to my mind is that I have the grace to be a member of the household of the true faith the Church of Rome will always be for a reflecting human being. Aren't we told by the divine psalmist that we should "Shout for joy" at the thought of our being Catholics? I know these words are taken in their accomodated sense, but what is the harm in making use of everything in the Holy Scriptures to express the gratitude we owe to God for all we have received from His mercy and love, the gift of faith in the holy Roman Catholic Church constituting the highest of these gifts which can be received in the present life and it is only in the state of glory we will experience a happiness greater than the one we now have in the realization of our being the members of the only true Church. "Ah, you are beautiful, my love," we say to Christ, but we also address these words to the Church of Rome, for she too is endowed with the preciousness-from on high, and so to her too we repeat the words of the Song of Songs and say with the bride-soul, "Ah, you are beautiful, my lover—yes, you are lovely" (Song of Songs 1:16). Are there any words more beautifully sweet than these with which to speak of the beauty of Christ's being and of the Church founded by Him?

There is a beauty in the Church and it is made manifest in the writings of the Fathers and Doctors of the Church as well as all the saints who have ever lived. Christ lives in the saints; they exemplify Him in their daily lives and with this exemplification there is a beauty to be found like in the angels and saints in heaven. The saints bring down this beauty on this earth for in them we get a living experience of what the beauty of the God Man was like. Do we wish to become beautiful with Christ's own beauty? If we do, it is to the Church of Rome we must go for that kind of beauty, a beauty to be found in everything she promulgates by way of her liturgy, her chants, her statutes and her paintings. It is to the Church of Rome we have to go to get a living experience of the beauty of Christ's being, seeing that that beauty of His is enshrined and interwoven with everything she does and is. There is a beauty from heaven to be had in the Church of Rome and it is found in the doctrines she promulgates.

And so, one can go on and on writing of all that the Church of Rome is and never come to end in his ceasing to praise all her divine qualities. Is she not the heavenly Jerusalem which has descended on this earth?

There is a need in the soul for the presence of God in His naked essence and not merely in His Sacramental one. And, though some people like to speak of the "historical Christ," it is Christ on the altar that matters so much for a member of the household of the true faith. For a member of the household of the faith it is Christ in His Eucharistic Presence the saints go to for warmth of heart and mind and the consolations they stand in need all the time they find themselves away from the home of the soul Christ is in the state of glory.

How joyous, how tremendously peaceful the hours have been that as a Jewish convert I have spent in prayer before the Blessed Sacrament! How sorry I feel for my fellow Jews who fail to have their God in that way in their own synagogues! Who is there who would want to go to a synagogue for the warmth of heaven's joys to be had in a Catholic Church? And, one may ask, what is a Church without Christ's Sacramental Presence in her? Is not that place nothing else but just another building? In ancient times God dwelt in the "ark." He does so today in the tabernacle on the altar, in the front of which a light burns to tell us that the Lord and Creator of the universe is there present in the Sacramental Presence of His Divine Son. Is this not enough to make a Jewish person dissatisfied with his synagogical form of worship?

Is there not a craving in the heart of a Jewish person for Christ the Lord as He may be had on this earth by means of the Holy Eucharist? What can any religion have to offer which cannot give us Christ in His Eucharistic Presence? So that when we go to the place where He is there present we get the feeling we will have when we shall be with Christ in the state of Glory, the state of Glory which has its beginning right here on this earth so as to enable us to "Taste and see how good [Hebrew: sweet] the Lord is" (Ps. 34:9). Christ is sweet to the souls of those who have the grace to have the thought of His Being deeply rooted in that part of themselves made in the Image of His Father in heaven. There is a sweetness of Christ to be experienced in the Church of Rome in which same He has deigned to take up His Blessed Abode, so that when we walk into a Church we get the feeling we are in the presence of those who are already in heaven, in the place of infinite bliss that name designates for a believing human being. For a believing human being, heaven denotes Christ the Lord, that word having Him alone in view.

I think of all this as I find myself praying before the Blessed Sacrament. I think of all this and as I do so, I am filled with compassion for the Jewish people who have no Christ on their altar to turn to for comfort in their innumerable earthly needs, for the kind of consolation to be had in Christ alone in His Eucharistic Presence.

Why don't men die of grief at the realization that they lack the faith to believe in the only true Church! How can the Jewish people endure being Jews and not Christians? How are they able to endure the lack of grace Christianity can alone supply them? It is Christ the Jewish people have to have for them to go through the sorrows of their earthly lot.

> Hear, O heavens, and listen, O earth,
> for the Lord speaks:
> Sons have I raised and reared,
> but they have disowned me!
> An ox knows its owner,
> and and ass, its master's manger;
> But Israel does not know,
> my people has not understood.
> (Is. 1:2-3)

It is of the Jewish people these words have been written, God foreseeing their sorrowful state for not knowing Him in the Person of His Son. I get a depressing feeling everytime I pass a synagogue, knowing Christ has now transferred His presence from that place to where He exists in His Sacramental state. I think of all this and a dreary feeling comes over me, and I pray for those who know not Christ in His Sacramental state, and their not knowing Christ in that state, they do not have the grace to love the Love Itself Jesus is. "Come to me, all you who are weary and find life burdensome, and I will refresh you" (Mt. 11:29) our Lord says to the Jewish people. . . .

How we should thank God for the fact that we are Catholics, so that we may in that way have Christ with us in the Church near where we live. As Catholics, we don't have to go far away to find Christ, seeing that in His Sacramental Presence he resides at our very doorsteps in the nearest Church we happen to find ourselves, so that to have heaven, all we have to do is to step inside, and make an act of faith in the Real Presence, seeing that in that way we can all rise to the heights of the most sublime kind of prayer it is in the province of a human being to be able to experience.

And although in the Old Testament God performed wondrous deeds, they're surpassed to an infinite degree in His making Himself available to us in the Holy Eucharist. What are the marvels performed by Moses compared to those performed by the priest during the act of consecration?

I know I am digressing. But is not our whole life a kind of digression, digression from our home in heaven to this sad earthly exile where we cannot experience what they do who have had the grace to depart from this life? We cannot be happy in the present life but only in the one to come, and it is in the realization of this truth that our sanctity consists. Our sanctity consists in the realization that it is only when we will be completely with Christ in the state of glory that in ourselves made in the image of God will attain full fruition and not until that blessed day. Until that blessed day we are going to remain the "foreigners" on this earth of which the psalmist speaks (Ps. 39:14).

With the saints, it is Jesus twenty-four hours of the day, or not to have Him in their inner being. The saint does nothing by halves, so his love for Christ falls into this category. Once we get the grace to love Christ, it is hard to have any love in our hearts for anything else God has made, be this good and beautiful as it may. The psalmist speaks of Christ being "Fairer in beauty.. ..than the sons of men" (Ps. 45:2) and it is this beauty of Christ's Being I fell in love with since the first day of my conversion. I feel sorry for my fellow Jews who fail to love the Love Itself Jesus is, and I shall never never fail to feel sorry for them on this account. A great Jewish convert, the Ven. Mary Paul Libermann, once wrote these words about someone in his family who was not a Catholic. So and so, he said, "is not a Catholic." So and so, he said, "is still a Jew, and therefore nothing." People may consider these harsh words, but to me, they have always spoken the deepest truths that can be uttered, seeing if we fail to love Christ, we are in the eyes of God nothing at all, seeing Christ constitutes the sole Reality this universe contains, at least, without Christ rooted in our deep inner being, we are nothing at all. In fact without faith in Christ nothing has any meaning, at least without faith in Him nothing this world contains has any relevance for eternity, and not having any relevance for the life to come, what is there on this earth worth taking seriously, seeing the sole reason why anything has any meaning for us is due to the fact that that thing is of a nature to last forever. If it is not of a nature to last forever, it is of no worth in the eyes of God, and not having any worth in the eyes of God, it has no worth in our own estimation either, so that the attitude we should have towards that thing is as if it had never existed.

I know that these are not the kind of thoughts which would be popular among a certain class of people. But these are the kind of thoughts which have been popular with every single man and woman who was blessed with the gift of faith in our divine Lord. These were the kind of thoughts which have been popular with the Patriarchs and Prophets of the Old Testament, seeing one of them went so far as to say that without faith in Christ it were better such a person had never been born (Eccl. 4:2-3).

We have not been put on this earth in order to get along with our fellow human beings. We have been put on it for the sole purpose of seeking the truth and to follow that truth no matter where it will lead us. In my case, the quest for God's truth led me to the feet of St. Peter in the City of Rome, so it is for this reason I have the grace to find myself a member of the Mystical Body of Christ. We are not born to become this or that; we are born to be the truth-seekers God wishes us to be, the Truth our Lord Himself said He was in the words, "I am the Way, the Life and the Truth." Once he has received the grace to become a Catholic, the life of a convert becomes a song he will sing for the rest of his earthly days, and this is especially true of converts from Judaism, seeing all such go from darkness to the light to be had in Christ alone.

"Sing to him [to the Lord] a new Song" (Ps. 33:3), we are told by the divine psalmist, this Song we sing when we get the grace to become Catholics. All others are in the category of those who said they cannot "sing a song of the Lord in a foreign land" (Ps. 137:4), the "foreign land" they were in prior to the gift of faith in the only true Church. And so, finding ourselves in the Church of Rome, we sing to the Lord the new Song He asks we should sing to Him, a Song having in itself the joy of heart which has been given him as a result of his new-found faith. And so, as a former member of Judaism, I sing this song with all those who are the recipients of a similar grace. With St. Paul we all say,

> It was through the law that I died to the law, to live for God. I have been crucified with Christ, and the life I live now is not my own; Christ is living in me. I still live my human life, but it is a life of faith in the Son of God, who loved me and gave himself for me. I will not treat God's gracious gift as pointless. If justice is available through the law, then Christ died to no purpose.
> (Gal. 2:19-21)

I have passed my eighty-seventh year, so where do we go from here? My "bags are packed," they have been packed since the first day I became a Catholic. Since the first day I became a Catholic I had only one thought: What am I doing in a world like this, so far away from the homeland of my soul Heaven is? The gates of heaven having been opened up for me by my baptism, why stand outside like a prodigal son? I listen to the music from heaven ringing in my inner hearing, so I long to be where this music comes from, in the angelic world where all the blessed souls now are and among them some of my dearest friends I had on this earth, two of whom were my Jesuit spiritual directors who are responsible for everything I now am in a spiritual way. I think of all this and as I do so I find myself drawing near the goal of my heart's desire Jesus in the state of glory is, so I wonder why am I being detained on this earth? But I realize God has His own reason for this kind of detention, so I say *Fiat* and with this word comes a peace of soul I would not exchange for all the wealth of the world. Still, in spite of the patience I have the grace to have from my having to be so far away from the home of the soul heaven is, I look forward to the "Day of the Lord" when I shall get the grace to enter into the kingdom of heaven for which we pray when we say, "Thy kingdom come." I think of all this and as I do so I call to mind the words in which the psalmist says, "Lead me forth from prison, that I may give thanks to your name" (Ps. 142:8). I too long to be set free from the prison of mortality so that with St. Paul I can be "freed from this life and be with Christ" (Phil. 1:23).

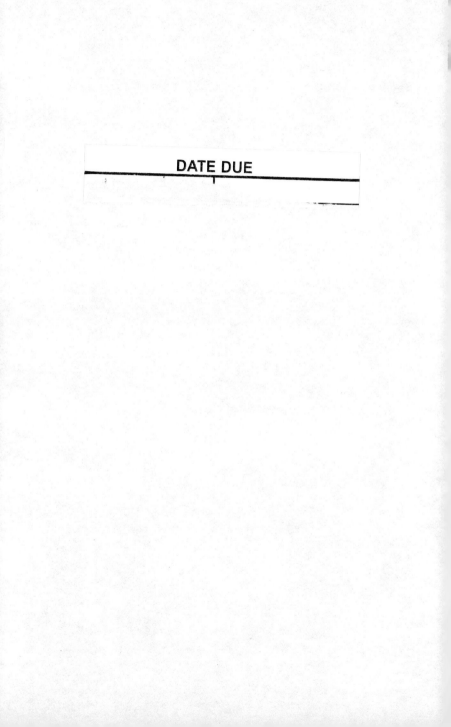
DATE DUE